## CONTENTS

| | |
|---|---|
| Fleet in Focus: Moss Hutchison   part 1 | |
| *Roy Fenton and John Cook* | 130 |
| Wreck of the *Holderness* | |
| *Graham Atkinson* | 142 |
| Photographer in Focus;  Tom Rayner | |
| *Tony Westmore* | 145 |
| Vessels broken up by Arnott Young at Dalmuir   part 2   *Ian Buxton* | 154 |
| Sources and acknowledgements | 164 |
| Scottish Shire Line,  part 1 | |
| *Ian Farquhar* | 165 |
| Overseas fruit ships in Hobart | |
| part 1   *Rex Cox* | 172 |
| An old Glen   *Richard Cornish* | 180 |
| Clan Line follow up | 182 |
| Putting the Record straight | 183 |
| Record reviews | 186 |
| Dr William Lind, Archivist extraordinaire, 1931-2007 | 188 |
| A Fort against the Rising Sun | |
| *Malcolm Cooper* | 190 |

**Ships in Focus Publications**

*Correspondence and editorial:*
Roy Fenton
18 Durrington Avenue
London SW20 8NT
020 8879 3527
rfenton@rfenton.demon.co.uk

*Orders and photographic:*
John & Marion Clarkson
18 Franklands, Longton
Preston PR4 5PD
01772 612855
shipsinfocus@btinternet.com

© 2008 Individual contributors, John Clarkson and Roy Fenton. All rights reserved. No part of this publication may be reproduced, stored in a retrieval system or transmitted in any form or by any means, electronic, mechanical, photocopying, recording or otherwise, without the written permission of the publisher.
Printed by Amadeus Press Ltd., Cleckheaton, Yorkshire.
Designed by Hugh Smallwood, John Clarkson and Roy Fenton.
SHIPS IN FOCUS RECORD
ISBN 978-1-901703-85-6

## SUBSCRIPTION RATES FOR RECORD

Readers can start their subscription with any issue, and are welcome to backdate it to receive previous issues.

| | 3 issues | 4 issues |
|---|---|---|
| UK | £24 | £31 |
| Europe (airmail) | £26 | £34 |
| Rest of the world (surface mail) | £26 | £34 |
| Rest of the world (airmail) | £31 | £41 |

# SHIPS IN FOCUS
## March 200

In this editorial we tell a little story about how Shire Line was written and developed. The spark was the composite photograph of six of the line's ships which appeared in the feature on photographer David de Maus in 'Record' 36. It was clear there was good photographic coverage of at least some of the company's ships, and the story was a natural follow-up to our recent book on Clan Line, a company which fully acquired Scottish Shire Line in 1918. Ian Farquhar produced an excellent history, focussing on the line's involvement in the Australasian frozen meat trade in which it became well known, and which undoubtedly proved the attraction to the Cayzers with their ambition to reinforce their Australian business. The fleet list originated with a draft kindly supplied by Bill Harvey, which was elaborated using closed registers in the National Archives and other sources. There was valuable input from Malcolm Cooper, who had data on Glasgow registrations, and Bill Schell, whose 'Registers' are always a source of accurate data. However, when Bill Schell saw a copy of what was fondly believed to be the final list, he realised that at least two of the early ships owned by founder James Turnbull had been missed, and identified *Renfrewshire* and *Lanarkshire*.

The omission occurred because it is difficult to be sure what ships a company owned prior to the late 1870s. This was when 'Lloyd's Register' first began to include lists of ship owners and their vessels, this list being the first resort of the fleet list compiler. It was believed that the first ship of Turnbull and his erstwhile partner Edward Martin was the secondhand *Sandringham*, which seemed reasonable given that most ownerships began with 'used' ships. *Renfrewshire* and *Lanarkshire* entered the fleet in the early 1870s and quickly left again, and it was not suspected that Turnbull started with new ships and quickly sold them. With deadlines looming and the National Archives closed for rebuilding, Malcolm Cooper was asked for registration details of the two extra vessels. It turned out that the *Lanarkshire* had been first registered in the names of James Turnbull, Emil Salvesen and Edward Martin. This not only put an earlier date on the Turnbull and Martin partnership than had been suspected, but indicated the involvement of a member of the well-known Leith shipping dynasty. Shown the details, Ian Farquhar looked in Vamplew's history of the latter concern, 'Salvesen of Leith'. Here was much more about the beginnings of Turnbull's ship owning, and confirmation that *Renfrewshire* was indeed his first steamer.

The moral of this tale is that co-operation between a number of shipping historians (very freely given, and much expedited in this case by the use of e-mail) can result in a much fuller picture emerging. And, for the editor who sat in the middle, it was a very satisfying and enlightening experience!

John Clarkson                                                                                                    Roy Fenton

Moss Hutchison's *Kantara* of 1925. See page 140 onwards. *[Harry Stewart/J. and M. Clarkson]*

**Fleet in Focus**

# MOSS HUTCHISON: Part 1
### Roy Fenton and John Cook

Of the major British liner companies operating post-war, few have been as badly neglected in published histories as the Moss Hutchison Line Ltd. of Liverpool. A short account of what is known about its origins is in order as a preliminary to a survey of the ships the company owned.

**James Moss**

The older of the two constituents was that founded by James Moss of Liverpool (1794-1849), whose father and uncle had been shipowners, agents and merchants in the West Indies trade. James first entered into a partnership with Theodor Cosack and they loaded their first vessel in 1820. They concentrated on sending salt to Danzig and some of the other ports in the lower Baltic, together with plantation goods such as sugar, tobacco and coffee. Three years later Moss decided to focus on the Italian trade so the partnership was dissolved and Cosack continued with the Baltic vessels. Thomas Hampson then joined Moss and the two built up a considerable business trading to western Italian and Levantine ports. This partnership lasted until 1833 when Hampson retired and James took his nephew William Miles Moss and a close personal friend, Richard Spencer, as partners. Steam ships were introduced to Liverpool's Mediterranean trade in 1845 but they were operated by London and Glasgow concerns and, within a few years, were making serious inroads into the Liverpool traders' business. William Miles Moss, just before his uncle's death, took the initiative and invited the principal local shipowners who were interested in the Mediterranean trade to a dinner at his house where he invited them to join him in investing in a steamship which he had just ordered from Alexander Denny of Dumbarton. As a result there was a close working relationship between James Moss and Co., John Bibby Sons and Co., Lamport and Holt, and Vianna, Chapple and Co.

Immediately after the Crimean War a service was started in conjunction with the young Alfred Holt to Bordeaux and Nantes but cotton from Egypt became the major cargo, especially during the American Civil War when supplies from the Confederacy were greatly restricted. Additional supplies were brought from Bombay and - before the opening of the Suez Canal - shipped to Suez and carried overland to Alexandria where Moss steamers loaded it for Liverpool. A seasonal service to the St. Lawrence was introduced and the Mediterranean services were expanded to include Syrian, Greek, Turkish and Black Sea ports. Frederick Leyland's takeover of the Bibby shipping operations in January 1873, following the death of William Miles Moss just over a year earlier, ended the cosy working arrangement in Liverpool's Mediterranean trade and the Moss family had to adopt limited liability to contain the risk faced by non-working family members and outside shareholders. The title Moss Steamship Co. Ltd. was adopted for the shipowning company, with management remaining in the hands of James Moss and Co. Most of the Moss steamers had always carried a few passengers but to winter in Egypt became a fashionable habit in the late Victorian era and so vessels were built with first class accommodation and a regular service was established to Alexandria: it only ceased when the ships were sunk during the First World War. By then Ellerman had bought Leyland's and Papayanni's fleets and Furness, Withy purchased 50% of Johnston's in 1914 with an option on the remaining 50%, and took a majority holding in Knott's Prince Line in August 1916. Cunard's Mediterranean services were, of course, just a small part of what had become a major diversified group, so, as the remaining independent, Moss must have felt increasingly isolated and vulnerable. The capital cost of replacing war losses must have also weighed heavily with them so an offer from the Royal Mail Group of £1,245,760 for both the owning and management companies was accepted in November 1916.

**J. and P. Hutchison**

Hutchisons was formed in 1859 when John Hutchison of Glasgow took a formerly bankrupt shipping agent, Thomas Brown, into partnership. Peter Hutchison joined the partnership a couple of years later by which time Hutchison and Brown had established a strong working relationship with Palgrave, Murphy and Co. of Dublin (this was to continue for over 100 years), and T. and J. Harrison had appointed them their Glasgow agents for the Charente wine and brandy boats. The initial service was from Glasgow and Dublin to Bordeaux and Nantes but a sailing ship service to Natal was run for a decade and, in 1863, an attempt was made to operate a service to Rio de Janeiro, Montevideo and Buenos Aires via Liverpool but the wrong ship was chosen, the voyage took nine months and Lamport and Holt proved to be much more professional! Hutchisons' ships proved much more suitable to the shorter-run continental routes and these were expanded to include Le Havre and Rouen, and into the Mediterranean to Barcelona, the Spanish fruit ports, Marseilles and Oran. 1868 saw the dissolution of the original partnership and J. and P. Hutchison came into being on 2nd March. Brown went on to fail for a second time by trying to run vessels in competition. A new service to Galway, Limerick and the west coast of Ireland was started in 1879; Hutchisons' steamer sailing the day after one owned by the Clyde Shipping Co., who eventually purchased the goodwill of Hutchisons' service in 1936. During the Franco-Prussian War the Hutchisons carried medical supplies for the French army free of charge and as a gesture of appreciation were allowed to use the French tricolour, defaced by a Scottish thistle, as their house flag. Other companies had been granted a similar privilege after the Crimean War but were asked to reverse the colours when the extent of their profits became known! In 1887 a new service to Stettin and Danzig was introduced which was later extended to Libau, Riga, Revel and St. Petersburg. John had died in 1883 and Peter bought out his family's share, later bringing his own son Thomas and a long-serving employee, John Gaff, into the business as junior partners. Peter died in 1899 and Gaff left in 1910 with £66,500 to start his own business. Although a

# Flags and funnels

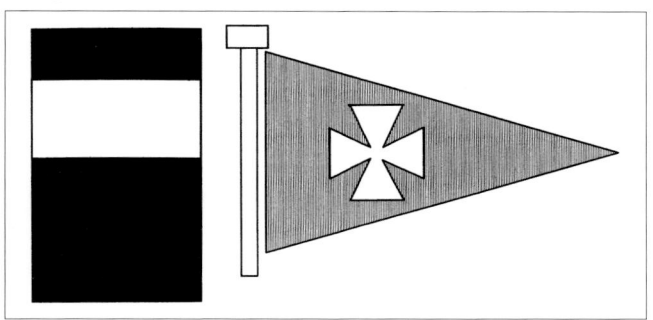

James Moss and Co. and the Moss Steamship Co. Ltd. The flag had a red background.

J. and P. Hutchison Ltd. The tricolour was red, white and blue (reading from the hoist) and the Scottish thistle was green.

Below: a fine piece of advertising for the Canadian services of the Moss Steamship Co. Ltd. The ship depicted is the *Meroe* of 1911, built at Middlesbrough, which was torpedoed and sunk by *U 63* off Cape Trafalgar on 29th October 1916 when homeward bound from Alexandria to Liverpool [Geoff Holmes collection]

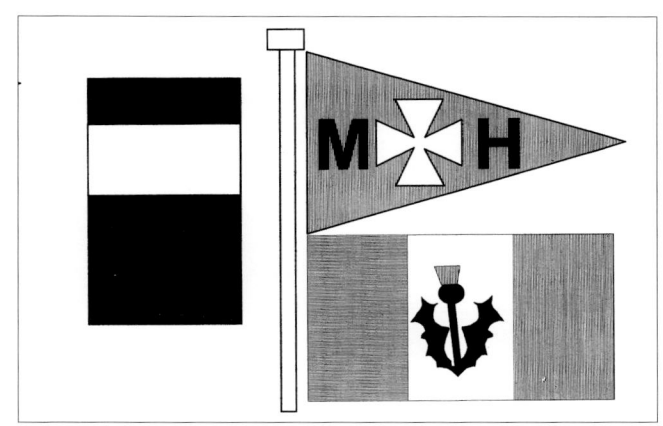

Moss Hutchison Line Ltd.
From April 1934 on the Mediterranean service only, both flags were flown. The letters on the red pennant were white.

number of Hutchisons' vessels were requisitioned during the First World War, the earnings of the others were so high that Thomas was able to purchase a majority holding in the Ailsa Shipbuilding Co. Ltd. of Troon in 1917 but he died the following year and his trustees felt that his son James (born 1893) was too young and inexperienced to control the businesses. An offer of £950,000 for 95% of the capital from the Royal Mail Group was too good to turn down - James was to retain 5% and become a non-executive director. As it turned out the company was sold at the very height of the market but not so Ailsa which Pirrie refused to buy and so the family retained it for many years until it was sold for a nominal £1 to British Shipbuilders. Although the shares in J. and P. Hutchison Ltd. were transferred to the Moss companies there was little rationalisation and the two concerns operated almost independently, the only discernable change being the adoption of Egyptian names for new Hutchison vessels rather than those of Greek heroes which had been used previously. It was at this

131

time that Palgrave, Murphy and Co. were winding down their operations and Hutchisons purchased the goodwill of their services to Oporto and Cadiz, and from the Bristol Channel to Hamburg, the latter being run in conjunction with Bugsier.

As a result of the Royal Mail financial crisis, the Moss and Hutchison companies were placed in voluntary liquidation in April 1934 and the following month the liquidator sold the assets to the newly-formed Moss Hutchison Line Ltd., which was immediately placed on the market. A certain amount of interest was shown by Andrew Weir who owned MacAndrews but it was the General Steam Navigation Co. Ltd., itself a part of the P&O Group, which was successful, paying a total of £458,213 in October 1935. This was little more than the written-down book value of the ships and was almost exactly half the sum paid by Royal Mail for Hutchisons alone.

Part 1 of this survey covers the ships which came from the two constituents of Moss Hutchison Line Ltd. Part 2 will feature ships acquired from elsewhere and those built post-war.

### Hutchison survivors
**ENDYMION**
*John Fullerton and Co., Paisley, 1909; 887g, 210 feet*
*T. 3-cyl. by Ross and Duncan, Glasgow*
*Endymion* only just qualifies for inclusion here, as she was sold to Gibraltar owners without change of name only a few months after the amalgamation. Her new career was short and tragic: on 31st January 1938 she was torpedoed by the Spanish Nationalist submarine *General Sanjurio* whilst on a voyage from Newport to Cartagena with a cargo of coke. [Roy Fenton collection]

**MEMPHIS** (1) (above and opposite top)
*Ardrossan Dry Dock and Shipbuilding Co. Ltd., Ardrossan, 1909; 1,032g, 200 feet*
*T. 3-cyl. by William Beardmore and Co. Ltd., Coatbridge, Glasgow*
This ship was built as *Smerdis*, but she disgraced herself and her name. On 16th December 1922 *Smerdis* fouled an anchor cable, capsized and sank in the River Mersey at the end of a voyage from Bordeaux with cargo which included iron ore. She was refloated in January 1923 and, although declared a constructive total loss, was repaired and returned to service, but now as *Memphis*.

In 1938 *Memphis* was sold to Moroccan owners as *Caïd-Kebir*, remaining under the same flag when sold again to become *Meziane* in 1954. Her end began in April 1955 when she sank alongside the quay at Rouen, after being struck by a lighter. Refloated, she was abandoned to the French government who sold the remains to Dutch breakers, who took delivery of her in 1957. [Harry Stewart/J. and M. Clarkson]

**PHILOTIS** (below)
*Ardrossan Dry Dock and Shipbuilding Co. Ltd., Ardrossan, 1917; 786g, 200 feet*
*T. 3-cyl. by William Beardmore and Co. Ltd., Coatbridge, Glasgow*

The sale of Moss Hutchison to General Steam in 1934 was clearly followed by some rationalisation of routes, as the new owner already had services to France. Inevitably there was then a clear out of the older ships. *Philotis* was sold to British and Continental in 1935, and under her new name *Nyroca* she was featured on page 74 of 'Record' 38. Fitting an oil engine in 1956, when she was already almost 30 years old, considerably prolonged her life and she lasted in Greek ownership as *Alice Marie* and later *Mairoula* until 1974 when broken up at Perama. She appears to be a sister of *Memphis*, although built eight years later. *[J. and M. Clarkson]*

**CHLORIS (1)** (top)
*Werft Nobiskrug G.m.b.H., Rendsburg, Germany, 1921; 1,193g, 250 feet*
*T. 3-cyl. by Ottensener Mach. G.m.b.H., Altona, Germany*
In the Hutchison fleet with some unusual, not to say slightly eccentric, designs, *Chloris* stood out, her bipod masts being unusual for a coaster in the 1920s (although there is another example featured elsewhere in this issue, *Holderness*). She had been built as *Eider* for Bugsier Reederei und Bergungs A.G. of Hamburg and was bought in 1923 when barely two years old. This was another ship not long to outlive the amalgamation, as she was sold in 1935 to Swedish owners to become *Venern*. She did, however, achieve old age. In 1954 she went to Greek owners resident in Alexandria who put her under the then-fashionable Costa Rican flag and renamed her *Angeliki*. A sale in 1959 saw her registered in Ethiopia, although renaming her *Ionian* in 1964 suggests that there was a Greek owner involved. She was last reported, derelict and abandoned, in the Somali port of Berbera in 1973. *[J. and M. Clarkson]*

**ARDENZA**
*Hawthorn and Co. Ltd., Leith, 1920; 933g, 210 feet*
*T. 3-cyl. by Hawthorn and Co. Ltd., Leith*
Completed for Thomas C. Steven and Co., Edinburgh, *Ardenza* was acquired by J. and P. Hutchison Ltd. in 1924 (upper middle) when the Edinburgh company could not pay its way. Not renamed, surprisingly, she gave 22 years' service, and could even find new owners in 1946 in the shape of Cory Brothers and Co. Ltd., Cardiff who renamed her *Cory Freighter* (bottom). A further sale in 1952 saw her becoming the Spanish *Atlante*. On 9th August 1957 she stranded on Les Bouefs Rocks, Nourmoutier Island whilst on a voyage from Huelva to Nantes with a cargo of copper ore. Her crew were rescued and a month or so later *Atlante* was refloated, but repair was uneconomic and she was taken to Nantes to be scrapped. *[B. and A. Feilden/J. and M. Clarkson (2), Roy Fenton collection]*

**PROCRIS** (top)
*A. and J. Inglis, Ltd., Pointhouse, Glasgow, 1924; 1,320g, 220 feet*
*T. 3-cyl. by A. and J. Inglis Ltd., Pointhouse, Glasgow*
Almost alone of Moss Hutchison's pre-war fleet, *Procris* was to serve her full term with the company, and when sold went straight to breakers at Port Glasgow where she was demolished in April 1951. *[Harry Stewart/J. and M. Clarkson]*

**FENDRIS** (middle)
*A. and J. Inglis Ltd., Pointhouse, Glasgow, 1925; 1,309g , 228 feet*
*T. 3-cyl. by A. and J. Inglis Ltd., Pointhouse, Glasgow*
*Fendris* also came through the war, and remained in the fleet until 1950 when sold to Hans Krüger G.m.b.H., Hamburg who renamed her *Annemarie Krüger*. She was broken up in Hamburg during 1960. *[R.J. Scott]*

**SMERDIS** (bottom)
*London and Montrose Shipbuilding and Repair Co. Ltd., Montrose, 1920; 815g, 189 feet*
*T. 3-cyl. by William Beardmore and Co. Ltd., Glasgow*
Photographed in May 1933, *Smerdis* had been acquired in 1927, having previously carried the names *Marion Merrett* and *Kirkwynd*. She was also to have a very brief career with Moss Hutchison. Ownership was formally changed in May 1934 but she was sold to Elder, Dempster Lines Ltd. in July and soon renamed *Ilorin*. Like *Endymion*, her end was brutal: on 1st September 1942 *Ilorin* was torpedoed and sunk by the German submarine *U 125* whilst on a voyage from Lagos to Takoradi. There were no survivors from her crew of 30. *[John McRoberts/J. and M. Clarkson]*

## SARDIS
*Ardrossan Dockyard Co. Ltd., Ardrossan 1928; 970g, 221 feet*
*T. 3-cyl. by J.G. Kincaid and Co. Ltd., Glasgow*

*Sardis* had a good set of derricks, but with her counter stern and an open bridge looks anachronistic for a 1928-built ship. She is seen on the Avon with the plain black funnel worn in her six years in Hutchison ownership (top) and with the white band added to her funnel after the amalgamation in 1934 (middle). It would be interesting to know just when her bridge was enclosed.

Sold to Spanish owners in 1950, *Sardis* still had almost 20 years of work ahead of her, all with her original engines. She was not renamed until 1954 when she became *Marichu*, but following sale to Greece in 1965 she had three names in just four years: *Phloisvos*, *Capo Pala* and *Agios Nicolaos*. It was fortunate that under the last of these names she was photographed in a Mediterranean port (bottom). She was broken up at Piraeus in 1969. *[Roy Fenton collection; J. and M. Clarkson; Roy Fenton collection]*

**BUSIRIS (1)** (above)
*Ailsa Shipbuilding Co. Ltd., Troon, 1929; 943g, 215.7*
T. 3-cyl. by the Ailsa Shipbuilding Co. Ltd., Troon

Built just a year later than *Sardis*, *Busiris* looks a little more modern, but still has an open bridge. A photograph taken after her 1948 sale to Monroe Brothers as *Kyleglen* shows that a wheelhouse was eventually fitted (middle). The aerial view emphasises the somewhat unusual arrangement of hatches, with two ahead of the bridge and one on her raised quarter deck. *Kyleglen* was broken up at Dublin in 1958. *[B. and A. Feilden/J. and M. Clarkson; Roy Fenton collection]*

## Moss survivors

**ASSIOUT** (below)
*North of Ireland Shipbuilding Co. Ltd., Londonderry, 1918; 4,215g, 370 feet*

Two steam turbines geared to one shaft by the British Westinghouse Electrical and Mechanical Co. Ltd., Manchester

The older Moss ships were not to remain in the combined fleet for long. *Assiout* was sold to Greece in 1935 and renamed *Maroulio*, later sold again as *Amarylis*, and placed under the Panama flag. She was torpedoed and sunk by *U 181* on 2nd December 1942 approaching Durban with a cargo of phosphate from Kosseir. *[M. Cooper/J. and M. Clarkson]*

**AMARNA** (top)
*North of Ireland Shipbuilding Co. Ltd., Londonderry, 1919; 4,195g, 370 feet*
*Two steam turbines geared to one shaft by British Westinghouse Electrical and Mechanical Co. Ltd., Manchester*
Londonderry-built sisters *Amarna* and *Assiout* were unusual for liner trade ships with their long bridge decks, and they were unique in the Moss Hutchison fleet for having turbine machinery. Their photographs here probably predate the amalgamation, as both ships were quickly sold, *Amarna* becoming the Greek *Efthalia Mari* in 1935. Like her sister, she was to meet a violent end: torpedoed and sunk by *U 177* on 5th August 1943 soon after leaving Lourenço Marques on a voyage to Alexandria with coal.
*[Harry Stewart/J. and M. Clarkson]*

**LANDES** (opposite middle)
*Hawthorns and Co., Ltd., Leith, 1920; 1,276g, 245 feet*
*T. 3-cyl. by Hawthorns and Co., Ltd., Leith*
Landes was quickly sold following the amalgamation, going to Finska Ångfartygs A/B, Helsinki as *Leo*. During the Fenno-Russian War she was bombed and sunk at Turku on New Year's Day, 1940, but refloated and repaired. By 1945 she was registered in Tallinn as *Gatchina* and survived into the 1970s before being broken up, although latterly she was used as a storage barge. *[National Maritime Museum, N43377]*

**LORMONT (1)** (opposite bottom)
*Hawthorns and Co., Ltd., Leith, 1920, 1,276g, 245 feet*
*T. 3-cyl. by Hawthorns and Co., Ltd., Leith*
Lormont joined her sister *Landes* in the same Finnish ownership, Finska Ångfartygs A/B, Helsinki. Renamed *Juno*, she was also to become an early war loss, mined and sunk on 30th October 1939 south east of Flamborough Head whilst northbound from London to Blyth and Vipuri with general cargo. *[B. and A. Feilden/J. and M. Clarkson]*

**HATASU** (above)
*John Blumer and Co. Ltd., Sunderland, 1921; 3,198g, 353 feet*
*T. 3-cyl. by John Dickinson and Son Ltd., Sunderland*
On 2nd October 1941 *Hatasu* was torpedoed and sunk by *U 431* some 600 miles east of Cape Race whilst on a ballast voyage from Manchester to New York. *Hatasu* had lost touch with convoy ON19, and losses amongst her complement of 47 were heavy. One boat did get away but, after 15 days adrift in severe weather in the North Atlantic, only six men survived to be rescued by a Unites States destroyer. *[B. and A. Feilden/J. and M. Clarkson]*

**KANTARA** (below)
*Barclay, Curle and Co. Ltd., Glasgow, 1925; 3,237g, 331 feet*
*T. 3-cyl. by J.G. Kincaid and Co. Ltd., Glasgow*
Kantara had the misfortune to be one of four ships sunk by the German battleship *Gneisenau* on 22nd February 1941 when their convoy dispersed east of Greenland. Her crew became prisoners-of-war and were transferred to the supply ship *Ermland*. Kantara was on a voyage from London and the Tyne to Barbados, Trinidad and Demerara with general cargo. *[B. and A. Feilden/J. and M. Clarkson]*

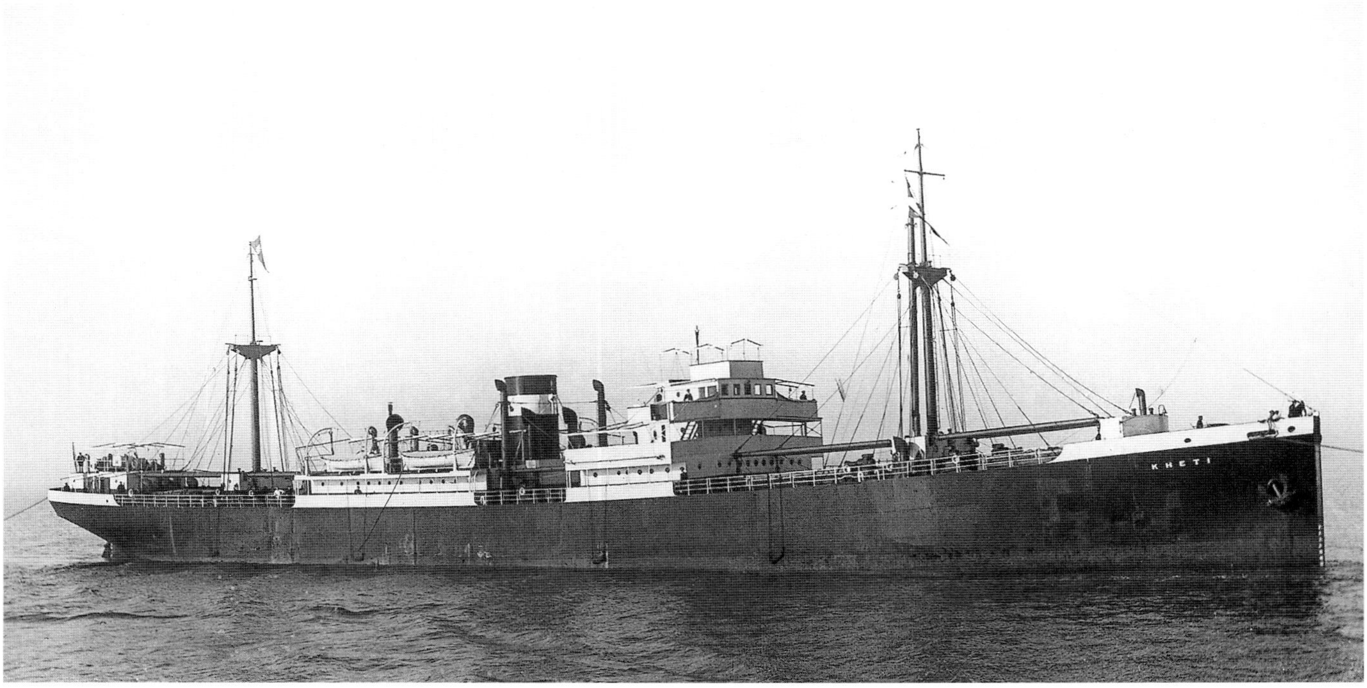
KHETI

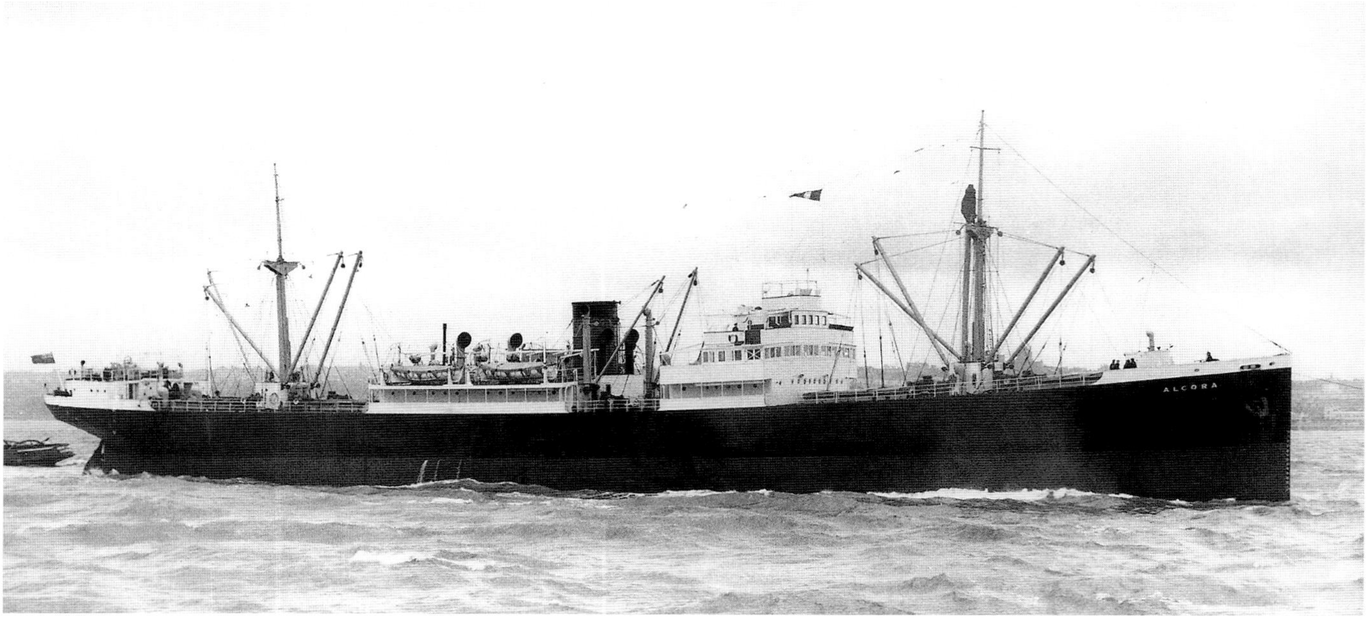
ALCORA

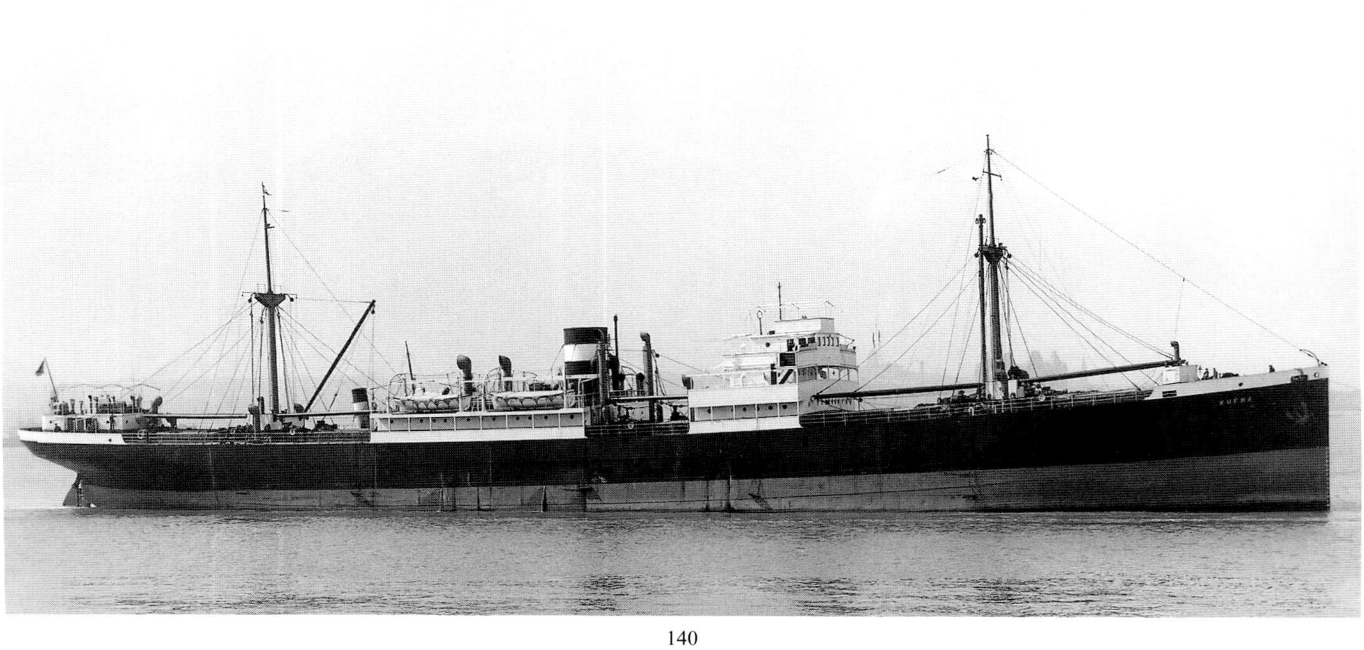

**KHETI** (opposite, top)
*Harland and Wolff, Ltd., Greenock, 1927; 2,734g, 331 feet*
*Oil engine 4SCSA 8-cyl. by Harland and Wolff, Ltd., Glasgow*

As did other companies controlled by Kylsant, Moss ordered several motor ships from Harland and Wolff Ltd. in the late 1920s, although - again like others for the group - they were under-powered for the liner trade, capable of only just over 11 knots.

With new motor ships arriving, *Kheti* (upper) was sold in 1951 and found a British buyer, John Bruce and Co. for whom she was owned by the Mossgiel Steamship Co. Ltd. as *Alcora* (middle). A further sale in 1958 saw her take a name that would be unlikely to be used now, *Gay Med*. Her last years, from 1964, saw her owned in Beirut but managed from Malta as *Med Star*. She foundered 9th October 1967, about 30 miles south of Pantelleria whilst bound from La Goulette via Malta to Bayonne with phosphates. *[Both: Roy Fenton collection]*

**KUFRA** (opposite bottom)
*Harland and Wolff, Ltd., Glasgow, 1929; 2,724g, 331 feet*
*Oil engine 4SCSA 8-cyl. by J.G. Kincaid and Co. Ltd., Greenock*

The second motor ship built for Moss, *Kufra* was unfortunate to become one of only two marine casualties that Moss Hutchison sustained during the fleet's 44 years, and even then wartime conditions contributed to the losses. On 24th June 1940 she was in collision with the French steamer *San Diego* (6,013/1930) in the Bay of Biscay whilst on a ballast voyage from Port Talbot and Verdon to Bayonne. *[B. and A. Feilden/J. and M. Clarkson]*

**KANA** (above)
*A. McMillan and Son, Ltd., Dumbarton, 1929; 3,743g, 333 feet*
*T. 3-cyl. by David Rowan and Co. Ltd., Glasgow*

After the two motor ships, Moss reverted to steamers with *Kana* and her sister *Kavak* from Dumbarton. *Kana* was the last of the pre-war ships to be sold, outlasting the motor ship *Kheti* by a year, going in 1952 to Italian owners as *Teresa Vigo*. In 1960 she became *Maria Piro* and in 1965 hoisted the Panama flag for owners in Trieste who gave her the distinctly un-Italian name *Old Oak*. She was broken up in Trieste during 1968. *[Geoff Holmes collection]*

**KAVAK** (below)
*A. McMillan and Son, Ltd., Dumbarton, 1929; 2,782g, 333 feet*
*T. 3-cyl. by David Rowan and Co. Ltd., Glasgow*

The steamer *Kavak* was torpedoed and sunk by *U 101* on 2nd December 1940 in the North Atlantic whilst on a voyage from Demerara to Newport, with a cargo of bauxite and pitch. *[John McRoberts/J. and M. Clarkson]*

*To be continued*

# WRECK OF THE HOLDERNESS
## Graham Atkinson

The slump which followed the boom just after the First World War brought the demise of many shipbuilders, one of which was the Rennie, Ritchie and Newport Shipbuilding Co. Ltd. The company owned two yards, one on the Clyde at Rutherglen and the other in Essex at Wivenhoe. Before it closed the Wivenhoe yard received an order for four ships. Three were completed as *Maindy Transport* (yard number 1309), *Maindy Tower* (1310), and *Maindy Keep* (1325) with the fourth, ordered as *Maindy Cottage*, completed as *Stockrington* (Yard No.1326) for Australian owners after the yard closed.

*Maindy Tower* was a short raised-quarterdeck type coaster with her bridge aft and was completed for Maindy Transport Co. Ltd. with Jenkins, Richards and Evans Ltd., Cardiff as her managers. Her dimensions were 207.5 x 33.6 x 13.5 feet and photographs of her later in her career show her with a set of goalpost masts at each end of her hold with a single derrick to each goalpost. Unusually for a steam coaster of this period she had an enclosed wheelhouse and at some point in her career another wheelhouse was constructed on top of the original, probably for better visibility over deck cargoes such as timber. Her triple-expansion steam engine was built by Plenty and Son Ltd., Newbury and was rated at 103 nominal horse power. The three cylinders had diameters 16.5, 27 and 30 inches with a stroke of 30 inches. Steam was raised in two single-ended boilers which had a working pressure of 180 psi.

In 1922 the South Wales colliery owner Sir David R. Llewellyn purchased *Maindy Tower* and her two sisters and the ships' managers became D.R. Llewellyn, Merrett and Price Ltd., Cardiff. All three ships regularly loaded South Wales coal for French ports and in 1924 *Maindy Keep* was lost on a voyage from Swansea to Bordeaux. The *Maindy Transport* and *Maindy Tower* were sold in 1925, the former becoming the *Ambleside* of Connell and Grace Ltd. of Newcastle-upon-Tyne. She went under the Latvian flag as *Livonia* in 1933, remaining managed by Connell and Grace, and in 1936 was sold to Norwegian owners to become *Lyng*. She was lost in an East Coast convoy collision during December 1942.

*Maindy Tower* was sold to John Geddes, Cullen, Banffshire and renamed *Gledburn*. Although based in Scotland her new owner chose Robinson, Brown and Co., Newcastle-upon-Tyne, as ship's managers in 1927 and the ship was registered in Newcastle. Before the Second World War her managers were the major coaster operator on the Tyne and their ships were heavily involved with the coal and fishing industries. Steam coal was loaded in north east ports for Scottish drifters based on the Scottish east coast as well as packed herrings for the Continent, returning with empty barrels during the herring season.

In 1932 Geddes took A.M. Couper as a partner in owning *Gledburn* and in 1934 Anthony and Bainbridge Ltd. of Newcastle were appointed managers. In 1936 *Gledburn* was sold to the 'Toft' Steamship Co. Ltd., managed by T.H. Donking and Sons Ltd. and she was renamed *Grangetoft*. T.H. Donking had originally been in partnership with R.A. Constantine to manage the Meteor Steamship Co. Ltd., formed in 1907. The two men had gone their own ways in 1923.

*Grangetoft* came through the Second World War although she sustained bomb and machine gun damage on 26th January 1941 when she was attacked by German aircraft in the Thames Estuary. In 1944 she took part in the Normandy Landings arriving from Portishead on 11th June at Utah Beach in Convoy EBC6W. On a later voyage to the beachhead she sustained bottom damage in bad weather and was beached at Utah Beach on 21st June where her cargo was discharged overside.

After the war the Donking fleet declined to a point where in 1955 only *Grangetoft* and *Dona Flora* (786/1924) were left. Both ships were sold to Holderness Steamship Co. Ltd., Hull and became *Holderness* and *Holdernett* respectively. Their new owner's company was formed in 1945 and had a policy of buying elderly steamships which were cheaper to buy than motor ships which meant smaller repayments on any mortgages against the ships. Steamers

Of the four ships built by Rennie, Ritchie and Newport Shipbuilding Co. Ltd. at Wivenhoe, all proved camera-shy except *Maindy Tower*, which was photographed under each of her names and guises. Opposite *Maindy Tower* in the Avon, right as *Gledburn*, below middle as *Grangetoft* under Donking ownership with the addition of an extra wheelhouse, and bottom *Holderness*. The bipod masts were an unusual feature on a British steam coaster of this period, and these and the twin derricks suggest the ships were designed for the liner trade. *[J. and M. Clarkson; Roy Fenton collection; World Ship Society Ltd., Ships in Focus]*

The wreck of *Holderness* at Blyth was readily visible from the pier. *[Author's collection]*

were actually good value as several together could make the same profit as a single motor ship but when the steamers needed surveys or expensive repairs they were sold, usually for demolition. Before she began trading for Holderness *Grangetoft* passed her special survey and was converted from coal to oil burning

On Wednesday 11th March 1959 *Holderness* sailed from Blyth at about 10.00 with coal for Londonderry. As she left the harbour mouth it is presumed that a combination of high winds and seas drove her onto Seaton Rocks, 50 yards from the East Pier Lighthouse. At first her stern faced the pier but eventually she drifted down the pier and was driven beam-on so that her bows now faced down the pier. The following day it was reported she had broken her back amidships and her cargo of coal was being washed out. Her forecastle eventually came to lie ten yards from the rest of the ship.

A few weeks later the local paper reported she had been abandoned as a total loss to Blyth Harbour Commissioners who would decide her fate, as had happened with Comben Longstaff's *Devonbrook* (803/1924) which had grounded in the same vicinity in 1946. Some demolition work was carried out but bottom plates of *Holderness* were left in situ and until recently could still be seen at low water.

## PHOTOGRAPHER IN FOCUS
# TOM RAYNER, 1921-1996
## Tony Westmore

Looking through any of the major serious shipping books published since the 1950s it will be difficult not to come across the name of Tom Rayner among the photo credits. The gentle exterior of a family man hid a passion for shipping and photography. Born in Ryde on the Isle of Wight in 1921, he came from a family that had no connection with the sea - his younger brother was to become a canon in the Anglican Church.

Tom's first encounter with ships took place on Ryde seafront as a youngster, watching the shipping movements in the then-busy Solent off Portsmouth. It was an aunt who encouraged Tom and was responsible for developing that interest, for it was she that would take him on early trips to Southampton to view the ships and where he started to photograph them. He saw war service with the Army as a military policeman and landed on the beaches in the D-Day landings. On leaving the Army he settled back to island life again, working for Woolworths in Ryde as their stockroom manager, contented with his lot; his spare time became increasingly involved with ships and photography. He continued to live in Ryde where he had met and married Isobel in 1944; they had a daughter Helen.

During regular forays to London and Liverpool he soon established contact with like-minded people and built up a series of contacts both at home and abroad, indeed friendship and overseas contacts ensured that the photographers of the day were able to swap and exchange negatives from the far corners to add to their individual collections. A friend of Michael Crowdy, Tom was a founder member of the World Ship Society, being a mainstay of the Isle of Wight Branch all his life. Among his close circle of friends were other well-known photographers of the time, John McRoberts, Alex Duncan, Len Sawyer and Roger Sherlock, and he was to spend many happy hours on the Thames and Mersey and in and around the docks in their company. His close ties with John McRoberts in Liverpool resulted in him obtaining his collection of glass plate negatives.

Photographic interests kept him busy but it was possibly in his dark room that he was in his element; here he could work and obtain the best possible print from a negative. He was to share these skills with both Alex Duncan and Roger Sherlock. He was heavily involved with the printing of the photos for many of the shipping publications of the day, the Wartime Standard Ship series by Bill Mitchell and Len Sawyer, in particular.

In the early sixties the local WSS branch had annual outings to the London Docks and, with an influx of young teenagers into the branch around this time, Tom's fatherly instincts together with his disciplinarian skills from Army days were sometimes stretched to keep the younger element of the party under control, especially on the long haul around the Royals. It is a tribute to Tom that among that bunch of raw youngsters from the Isle of Wight were some that were to make a name for themselves later, benefiting from Tom's enthusiasm, encouragement and sourcing of prints. Names that would later mature into researchers and authors in their own right, for Richard de Kerbrech, David Williams and David Hutchings all had much for which to thank Tom.

Unfortunately ill health, in the form of a degenerative disease, cut short Tom's love for his hobby and he was forced into taking early retirement in his early sixties. Ably nursed and cared for by his wife Isobel during the progressive deterioration in his health, he died in 1996 at the age of 75.

Family man Tom loved his garden and serious music, but was perhaps at his happiest when with his camera in the docks, or with his prints in his dark room. A member of local photographic clubs he produced a number of slide shows featuring life and scenes of the Isle of Wight, which still do the rounds today. His name will be long remembered, and it is good to think that his collection has passed into good hands and is regularly being used to illustrate the articles of this magazine today.

Tom heading down the Thames on the *Royal Sovereign* in 1953. *[F.R. Sherlock]*

### SAMARIA
*Cammell, Laird and Co. Ltd., Birkenhead, 1921; 19,848gt, 602 feet*
*Six steam turbines double-reduction geared to two shafts by Cammell, Laird and Co. Ltd., Birkenhead*

Apparently empty of passengers, an immaculate *Samaria* belies her 34-years in this superb photograph taken by Tom on 11th March 1955. Despite her appearance, she was less than a year away from the breakers, as she was sold to T.W. Ward Ltd. in January 1956 and broken up at Inverkeithing.

*Samaria* had begun her life on Liverpool to Boston sailings, but in 1951 was transferred to Cunard's Southampton to Quebec route.

### TWICKENHAM FERRY
*Swan, Hunter and Wigham Richardson Ltd., Newcastle-upon-Tyne, 1934; 2,839gt, 366 feet*
*Four turbines single-reduction geared to two shafts by Parsons Marine Turbine Co. Ltd., Newcastle-upon-Tyne*

Something of a contrast with the graceful *Samaria*, this train ferry shares her turbine-driven twin screws. Designed for the Dover to Dunkirk sailings of the Southern Railway, *Twickenham Ferry* was actually French manned under the ownership of the S.A. de Navigation Angleterre-Alsace-Lorraine, whilst her two sisters, *Hampton Ferry* and *Shepperton Ferry*, were British flagged. *Twickenham Ferry* was broken up in Spain during 1974.

**BOURNEMOUTH QUEEN**
*Ailsa Shipbuilding Co. Ltd., Troon, 1908; 429gt, 200 feet*
*C. 2-cyl. by Hutson and Sons Ltd., Glasgow*

It is almost inconceivable now that any ship could operate for almost half a century for the same owner, yet *Bournemouth Queen* did so. She was built in 1908 for the Southampton, Isle of Wight and South of England Royal Mail Steam Packet Co. Ltd. and at the very end of 1957 left Southampton for breakers at Ghent. Her service was interrupted by two world wars, however: in the first she was commissioned as the minesweeper HMS *Bourne* and in the second served as an anti-aircraft and later an accommodation ship.

In the background of Tom's photograph is a flying boat, possibly one of the Saunders Roe Princess craft which spent so long in lay up waiting for sufficiently powerful engines to be developed that the flying boat era passed and they were, sadly, broken up.

**CITY OF EXETER**
*Vickers-Armstrongs Ltd., Newcastle-upon-Tyne, 1953; 13,345gt, 541 feet*
*Two Doxford-type oil engines 6-cyl. 4SCSA by Hawthorn, Leslie and Co. Ltd., Newcastle-upon-Tyne*

Post-war Ellerman and Bucknall built four cargo-passenger ships for their service from London to South and East Africa. In 1971 all four were sold to the Karageorgis group for reconstruction as passenger and vehicle ferries. Given the scale, it is not surprising that only two were completed, one being *City of Exeter* which became the *Mediterranean Sea* and entered service between Patras and Ancona in 1972. She survived until 1998, for the last few years carrying the names *Tutku* and *Alice* before being broken up at Aliaga.

**BARON HERRIES**
*Lithgows Ltd., Port Glasgow, 1940; 4,574gt, 416 feet*
*T. 3-cyl. by David Rowan and Co. Ltd., Glasgow*
A classic view of a classic steam tramp: lighters work alongside *Baron Herries* on the Thames during 1956. Completed in the early months of the Second World War, the Hogarth tramp has a wooden bridge front, a frippery which austerity would not allow in ships laid down in wartime. Despite her basic triple expansion engines, *Baron Herries* tramped on for the Scottish owners until October 1960, when a Greek owner bought her and renamed her *Athos II*. A grounding in the entrance to the Bosphorus in March 1962 spelt the end for the ageing steamer, and three months later Turkish breakers set to work on her.

**CEDARPOOL**
*William Gray and Co. Ltd., Hartlepool, 1942; 7,019gt, 446 feet*
*T. 3-cyl. by Central Marine Engine Works, Hartlepool*
It is September 1956, and *Cedarpool* has a full deck cargo of army vehicles, loaded for Operation Musketeer, the invasion of Suez. She had been built at Hartlepool as *Empire Clarion* and was immediately placed under management of local owner Sir Robert Ropner and Co. Ltd. Indeed, bought and renamed *Cedarpool* in 1946 she spent her entire career under Ropner control, being sold straight to Hamburg breakers in July 1959.

**ESSO APPALACHEE**
*Furness Shipbuilding Co. Ltd., Haverton Hill-on-Tees, 1942; 9,819gt, 504 feet*
*T. 3-cyl. by Richardsons, Westgarth and Co. Ltd., Hartlepool*
This former Empire tanker has almost completed discharging at Fawley on 15th March 1952. *Empire Dickens*, as she was completed, was a 'Norwegian' type, so called because her design was based on two tankers built for Westfal-Larsen & Co. A/S of Bergen by Sir James Laing and Sons Ltd., Sunderland. The name *Esso Appalachee* was applied in 1946 when she was bought by Anglo-American Oil Co. Ltd., a company which took the more familiar name Esso Petroleum Co. Ltd. in 1947. *Esso Appalachee* went to breakers at Faslane in August 1960.

**HYRCANIA**
*Alabama Dry Dock and Shipbuilding Co., Mobile, USA, 1944; 10,644gt, 524 feet*
*Turbo-electric by General Electric Co., Lynn, Massachusetts, USA*
Although her name suggests Shell, the T2 tanker *Hyrcania* was actually owned by the Baltic Trading Co. Ltd. The former *Chatterton Hill* was bought by this independent tanker company in 1947, and was scrapped at Bilbao, still as *Hyrcania*, in 1983. The photograph was taken in July 1957.

**FERNVALLEY**
*Alexander Stephen and Sons Ltd., Linthouse, Glasgow, 1955; 4,440gt, 428 feet*
*Oil engine 4-cyl. 2SCSA by Alexander Stephen and Sons Ltd., Linthouse, Glasgow*
Photographed off Hook in July 1958, Fearnley and Eger's *Fernvalley* sports the funnel of the Scandinavian West Africa Line. The Scottish-built ship was sold to Greece in 1968 to become *Calliope L* and was broken up at Barcelona in 1980.

**GOOD HOPE CASTLE**
*Caledon Shipbuilding and Engineering Co. Ltd., Dundee, 1945; 9,881gt, 498 feet*
*Two steam turbines double-reduction geared to a single screw by Richardsons, Westgarth and Co. Ltd., Hartlepool*
The fast standard cargo liner *Empire Life* was assigned to management by T. and J. Harrison Ltd., but neither she nor her sister *Empire Captain* was bought by the Liverpool company. Instead *Empire Life* was sold in April 1946 to Union-Castle Mail Steamship Co. Ltd. and renamed *Good Hope Castle*. Unusually, but appropriately given her name, Union-Castle registered her at Cape Town. She was broken up in Hong Kong during 1959.

**GATLING**
*Lobnitz and Co. Ltd., Renfrew, 1945;
392gt, 145 feet
T. 3-cyl. by Lobnitz and Co. Ltd.,
Renfrew*
Gatling was one of five armament stores carriers built for the Admiralty by Lobnitz. Designed for service in the Pacific, but too late to take part in the war, they were intended to carry stores from ships at anchor to small harbours, and could take the ground if necessary. Gatling was sold to H.G. Pounds, Portsmouth in 1969.

**LUCERNE**
*Glommens M/V., Fredrikstad, 1946;
533gt, 148 feet
Oil engine 7-cyl. 2SCSA by Nydqvist & Holm A/B, Trollhattan*
The lack of a coastline has not deterred the Swiss from owning coasters, but these vessels are sufficiently rare to warrant inclusion of Lucerne in this feature. Given the height of her masts and superstructure, her timber deck cargo in this photograph did not come down the Rhine from her home port of Basle.

She had been built as *Bardal* for Norwegian owners, becoming *Lucerne* in 1951 when bought by Trafina S.A. She kept this name only until 1956, when began a long series of renamings: first to *Wolfram*, to *Bardal* again in 1964, to *Underas Sandtag V* in 1965, to *Sangard* in 1979, to *Sandstorm* in 1979 and to *Annika* in 1997. Under the Finnish flag she is still afloat, although lengthened and re-engined since photographed in August 1955.

**JOHN PERRING**
*William Beardmore and Co. Ltd., Coatbridge, 1926; 1,559gt, 267 feet*
*T. 6-cyl. by William Beardmore and Co. Ltd., Coatbridge*
John Perring's exterior state belies her cargo. The sludge vessel's role was to take the solid residue which remained after London's sewage had been treated at works at Cross Ness or Barking and dump it in the appropriately-named Black Deep. Hermetically sealed tanks ensured that not even a whiff of sewage was apparent. This London County Council vessel was transferred to the Greater London Council in the 1960s and broken up by T.W. Ward Ltd. at Inverkeithing in 1968.

**KENIA**
*Cochrane and Sons Ltd., Selby, 1927; 200gt,*
*T. 3-cyl. by Crabtree and Co. Ltd., Great Yarmouth*
Kenia was built for William Watkins Ltd., passing in 1950 to Ship Towage (London) Ltd. on the amalgamation of Watkins with the Elliot Steam Tug Co. Ltd. She had a passenger certificate for 200.

Her end was violent. On 12th October 1964 Kenia sank whilst handling the Dutch vessel *Maashaven* at Tilbury although fortunately she went down slowly enough to allow the crew to get ashore. Although raised, she was quickly sold to breakers at Sheerness.

**ROYAL DAYLIGHT**
*John Stewart and Sons Ltd., Blackwall, 1902; 83gt, 75 feet*
*C. 2-cyl. by John Stewart and Sons Ltd., Blackwall*

Tom's photographs provide a delightful record of the Thames lighterage industry which disappeared so quickly, as did so much of the London river shipping scene. On the 1st June 1953, the Esso tug has charge of two dumb barges, *Esso Montgomery* and *Esso Stafford*, and is in company with a steam collier and the Dutch motor coaster *Erna* (362/1940). The steam tug had been built for the Anglo-American Oil Co. Ltd. with the name *Tea Rose* and in 1906 was renamed *Royal Daylight* after an Esso brand. She was broken up in 1955.

**TYBURN BROOK**
*Henry Scarr Ltd., Hessle, 1950; 68gt, 68 feet*
*Oil engine by British Polar Engines Ltd., Glasgow*

No excuse is needed for including another lighterage tug, this time against a background clutter of sheds, Scotch derricks and repair facilities on 7th June 1952. *Tyburn Brook* was owned by River Lighterage Co. Ltd. of Brentford. She was sold to United Towing Co. Ltd., Hull in 1963 to become *Pressman*. In 1972 her next owner altered her name by just one letter to *Presstan*. She retained this name under a variety of owners on the Thames, Medway, in the Isle of Wight, at Grimsby and Hull until broken up at New Holland in 2004.

# VESSELS BROKEN UP BY ARNOTT, YOUNG AT DALMUIR
## Part 2: 1963-1980
### Ian Buxton

Tonnages given for merchant ships are gross, for warships displacement (shown as 'd').
All vessels are iron or steel steamers unless otherwise stated.
Where known, the final operator or navy is listed.

**CORINTHIAN**
Cargo 3,198/1938
Ellerman Lines Ltd., London
Purchase price £22,750
Arrived 5.4.1963
Hulk to Old Kilpatrick
First non-BISCO ship.

**TURK**
Puffer 70/1929
J. and J. Hay Ltd., Glasgow
Arrived 1.6.1963.

**CRAIGIEHALL**
Dredger 693/1903
Trustees of the Clyde Navigation
Purchase price £9,084
Arrived 6.8.1963.

**SAINT KENTIGERN**
Coaster 249/1938
J. and A. Gardner and Co. Ltd., Glasgow
Purchase price £1,500
Arrived 10.1963.

**CLAN MACAULAY**
Cargo 10,492/1936
Clan Line Steamers Ltd., London
Purchase price £77,490
Arrived 18.11.1963.

**TEXAN**
Puffer 71/1937
J. and J. Hay Ltd., Glasgow
Arrived 12.1963.

**SLAV**
Puffer 68/1932
J. and J. Hay Ltd., Glasgow
Arrived 12.1963.

**GAEL**
Puffer 70/1931
J. and J. Hay Ltd., Glasgow
Arrived 5.8.1964.

**GLENARAY**
ex *VIC 89* 1947
Puffer 96/1945
G. and G. Hamilton Ltd., Glasgow
Purchase price £600
Arrived 24.12.1964.

**CRETAN**
Puffer 72/1939
J. and J. Hay Ltd., Glasgow
Purchase price £500
Arrived 24.12.1964.

**INCA**
Puffer 72/1938
J. and J. Hay Ltd., Glasgow
Purchase price £500
Arrived 12.1964.

*Corinthian. [J. and M. Clarkson collection]*

*Clan Macaulay. [J. and M. Clarkson collection]*

The Clyde puffer *Inca* was typical of the many puffers scrapped in the 1960s. She had her 15 minutes of fame when she starred as the 'Maggie' in the film of the same name. *[World Ship Society Ltd./Roy Fenton collection]*

The Abdiel class fast minelayer HMS *Ariadne*. After commissioning in February 1944 she laid mines off Norway and was then sent to the Pacific where she worked off New Guinea. *[J. and M. Clarkson collection]*

HMS *Termagant* was a wartime-built destroyer that in 1953 underwent a limited conversion to a fast frigate. *[FotoFlite/J. and M. Clarkson collection]*

**GANSEY**
ex *Barrule* 1955, ex *Coe Jean* 1950, ex *Empire Factor* 1946
Coaster 410/1944
C.D. and C.M. Watterson, Castletown
Purchase price £3,850
Arrived 26.12.1964.

**CONISTER**
ex *Abington* 1921
Coaster 411/1920
Isle of Man Steam Packet Co. Ltd., Douglas
Purchase price £4,325
Arrived 27.1.1965 having left Douglas in tow 26.1.1965.

**ARIADNE**
Minelayer 2,650d/1943
Royal Navy
Purchase price £68,725
Arrived 14.2.1965 from Devonport
Hulk to Troon 4.6.1965.

**BRISSENDEN**
Frigate 1,175d/1943
Royal Navy
Purchase price £28,750
Arrived 2.3.1965 from Lisahally
Hulk to Old Kilpatrick 9.10.1965.

**WARLIGHT**
Puffer 137/1920
Light Shipping Ltd., Greenock
Purchase price £1,225
Arrived 31.5.1965.

**TEAZER**
Frigate 1,930d/1943
Royal Navy
Purchase price £42,057
Arrived 7.8.1965 having left Chatham in tow 4.8.1965
Hulk to Old Kilpatrick 9.12.1965.

**LOCH VEYATIE**
Frigate 1,435d/1946
Royal Navy
Purchase price £24,650
Arrived 12.8.1965 from Lisahally.

**TUMULT**
Frigate 1,930d/1943
Royal Navy
Purchase price £42,500
Arrived 25.10.1965 from Rosyth.

**TERMAGANT**
Frigate 1,930d/1943
Royal Navy
Purchase price £42,500
Arrived 5.11.65 from Lisahally.

**IRK**
Hopper barge 740/1911
Purchase price £8,000
Arrived 22.7.1966.

**BARFLEUR**
Destroyer 2,315d/1944
Royal Navy
Purchase price £42,776
Arrived 29.9.1966 having left Devonport in tow 26.9.1966.

**MACBETH**
ex *Ayrshire* 1946
Trawler 575/1938
Hellyer Brothers Ltd., Hull
Purchase price £5,450
Arrived 20.1.1967 having left Fleetwood 18.1.1967
Beached at Old Kilpatrick 7.3.1967.

The Battle class destroyer HMS *Barfleur* was the only one of class to see action during the Second World War. She joined the British Pacific fleet upon commissioning in 1944 and was present in Tokyo Bay when Japan's official surrender was signed in September 1945. *[J. and M. Clarkson collection]*

**PASS OF BALMAHA**
ex *Empire Damsel* 1947
Coastal tanker 784/1942
Bulk Oil Steamship Co. Ltd., London
Had been used as a hulk at Dundalk
Purchase price £6,500
Arrived 18.2.1967
Demolition commenced 8.3.1967.

**ROCKET**
Frigate 2,300d/1943
Royal Navy
Purchase price £48,000
Arrived 20.3.1967 having left Portsmouth 14.3.1967.

**CIRCE**
Minesweeper 1,010d/1942
Royal Navy
Purchase price £10,254
Arrived 12.4.1967 having left Lisahally in tow 10.4.1967.

**STONECHAT**
Minelayer 560d/1944
Royal Navy
Purchase price £4,557
Arrived 13.4.1967 from Lisahally.

**ESPIEGLE**
Minesweeper 980d/1942
Royal Navy
Purchase price £14,200
Arrived 14.4.1967 having left Lisahally in tow 13.4.1967.

**SAXON**
Puffer 64/1903
James W. Connell Ltd., Coatbridge
Arrived 8.6.1967 in tow of *Raylight* from Greenock.

**FINISTERRE**
Destroyer 2,315d/1945
Royal Navy
Purchase price £45,250
Arrived 12.6.1967 having left Devonport 9.6.1967.

**STARLIGHT**
Puffer 91/1937
Light Shipping Co. Ltd., Greenock
Purchase price £550
Arrived 12.7.1967 in tow of *Stormlight* from Greenock.

**CUMBRAE LASS**
ex *Texa* 1964, ex *Pibroch* 1957
Puffer 96/1923
William Burke, Greenock
Purchase price £550
Arrived 8.1967
Demolition commenced 14.8.1967.

**INVERCLOY**
Puffer 95/1934
G. and G. Hamilton Ltd., Glasgow
Arrived 23.10.1967.

**TALISMAN**
ex *Aristocrat* 1946, ex *Talisman* 1940
Excursion steamer 554/1935
Caledonian Steam Packet Co. Ltd., Glasgow
Arrived 17.10.1967.

**HOPPER No.7**
Hopper barge 842/1912
Trustees of the Clyde Navigation, Glasgow
Purchase price £4,700
Arrived 2.1968
Demolition commenced 8.3.1968.

**TANKITY**
ex *M.O.B. 7* 1957
Tank barge 145/1946
F.T. Everard and Sons Ltd., Greenhithe
Arrived 4.1968
Demolition commenced 10.5.1968.

**MADGE**
Steam lighter 187/1913
Liverpool Lighterage Co. Ltd., Liverpool
Purchase price £1,000
Arrived 24.4.1968
Resale from Northern Slipway, Dublin.

156

**P.M. COOPER**
ex *William Cooper* 1964, ex *Mersey No.37* 1963, ex *No.37* 1947, ex *Foremost 38* 1925
Hopper barge 775/1925
William Cooper and Sons Ltd., Liverpool
Purchase price £8,500
Arrived c28.5.1968 having left Liverpool 27.5.1968
Demolition commenced 25.6.1968.

**CROSBY DALE**
ex *Xanthus* 1959
Tank barge 213/1927
Thomas Routledge, Liverpool
Purchase price £2,500
Arrived 29.5.1968 having left Liverpool 27.5.1968
Demolition commenced 9.8.1968
Resale from Northern Slipway.

**STORM COCK**
Tug 171/1936
Liverpool Screw Towing Co. Ltd.
Purchase price £4,000
Arrived 2.7.1968 having left Liverpool in tow of *James Lamey* 1.7.1968
Demolition commenced 20.8.1968
Resale from Northern Slipway.

**NORTH COCK**
ex *Hornby* 1967
Tug 201/1936
Liverpool Screw Towing Co. Ltd.
Purchase price £4,000
Arrived 2.7.1968 having left Liverpool 1.7.1968
Demolition commenced 29.8.1968
Resale from Northern Slipway.

**MARSH COCK**
ex *Wapping* 1967
Tug 201/1936
Liverpool Screw Towing Co. Ltd.
Purchase price £4,000
Arrived 10.7.1968
Demolition commenced 6.9.1968
Resale from Northern Slipway.

**CROSBY**
Tug 215/1937
Alexanda Towing Co. Ltd., Liverpool
Purchase price £4,000
Arrived 10.7.1968
Demolition commenced 7.10.1968.

**ALFRED**
Tug 215/1937
Alexanda Towing Co. Ltd., Liverpool
Purchase price £4,000
Arrived 19.7.1968
Demolition commenced 3.10.1968
Resale from Northern Slipway.

**MSC ARCHER**
Tug 144/1938
Purchase price £1,250
Manchester Ship Canal Co. Ltd., Manchester
Arrived 19.7.1968
Demolition commenced 20.9.1968
Resale from Northern Slipway.

**SAMUEL HEWETT**
Trawler 589/1956
Heward Trawlers Ltd., London
Purchase price £7,657
Arrived 21.10.1968
Demolition commenced 31.10.1968.

A cross-section of the types of craft broken up at Dalmuir in the 1960s. Opposite the coastal tanker *Pass of Balmaha* (top), the puffer *Starlight* (middle) and the esturial tanker *Tankity* (bottom). This page shows the Clyde steamer *Talisman* (top), the dredger *P. M. Cooper* (middle) and the Liverpool tug *Crosby* (bottom). *[All: J. and M. Clarkson]*

**GLANMIRE**
ex *Lairdsbank* 1963
Coaster 814/1936
British and Irish Steam Packet Co. Ltd.,
Dublin
Purchase price £10,550
Arrived 4.1.1969.

**CLOCH LASS**
ex *Limelight* 1962, ex *VIC 23* 1948
Puffer 97/1942
William Burke, Greenock
Arrived 7.2.1969.

**CLEVELEYS**
Tug 110/1929
British Transport Docks Board, Fleetwood
Purchase price £2,200
Arrived 23.3.1969.

**BLACK COCK**
Tug 170/1939
Liverpool Screw Towing Co. Ltd.,
Liverpool
Purchase price £3,500
Arrived 25.3.1969.

**VECHT**
Dredger 141/----
Arrived 24.4.1969.

**SCHELDT**
Dredger 167/----
Arrived 24.4.1969.

**SEAWAY**
ex *Empire Palm* 1946
Tug 260/1942
Ardrossan Harbour Company, Ardrossan
Purchase price £3,500
Arrived 6.1969
Demolition commenced 1.7.1969.

*Black Cock* in Langton Lock, Liverpool. *[J. and M. Clarkson]*

**AH.6**
Hopper barge 270/1935
Ardrossan Harbour Company, Ardrossan
Arrived 6.1969 from Ardrossan.

**MELLITE**
Puffer 90/1889
Light Shipping Co. Ltd., Greenock
Arrived 19.8.1969.

**SPINEL**
ex *Empire Spinel* 1946, ex German 1945, ex *Spinel* 1940
Coaster 654/1937
William Robertson (Shipowners) Ltd.,
Glasgow
Purchase price £9,600.

Arrived 20.2.1970
Demolition commenced 11.3.1970.

**JACINTH**
Coaster 651/1937
William Robertson (Shipowners) Ltd.,
Glasgow
Purchase price £9,600
Arrived 9.3.1970
Demolition commenced 30.3.1970.

**CREMYLL**
Water carrier 244/1938
Ministry of Defence, London
Purchase price £4,500
Arrived 4.1970
Demolition commenced 17.4.1970.

*Spinel* arriving at Eastham. *[J. and M. Clarkson]*

**PORTWAY**
Dredger 298/1927
Holms Sand and Gravel Co. Ltd., Bristol
Purchase price £2,325
Arrived 17.4.1970
Demolition commenced 1.5.1970.

**CALEDONIA**
Excursion steamer 623/1934
Caledonian Steam Packet Co. Ltd., Glasgow
Arrived 5.1970
Resold to Charringtons for conversion to a restaurant on the Thames.

**TRAFALGAR**
Destroyer 2,325d/1945
Royal Navy
Purchase price £80,157
Arrived 7.7.1970 having been sold 8.6.1970.

**ZEST**
Frigate 2,300d/1944
Royal Navy
Purchase price £74,250
Arrived 8.1970 having been sold 24.7.1970
Hulk to Troon 8.4.71.

**PEAKDALE**
ex *Prinses Juliana* 1962
Sand dredger 507/1910
Richard Abel and Sons Ltd., Liverpool
Purchase price £7,250
Arrived 9.1970
Demolition commenced 20.9.1970
Resale from Northern Slipways.

**STAR**
Sand carrier
Purchase price £4,140
Arrived 9.1970.

**MURRAY**
Frigate 1,180d/1956
Royal Navy
Purchase price £31,250
Arrived 9.1970 having been bought 14.8.1970.

**ELEVATOR No.5**
Grain elevator
Possibly ex *M.O.T. Elevator No.5* 403/1954
Purchase price £5,750
Arrived 12.1970.

**HOPPER No.10**
Hopper barge 842/1912
Trustees of the Clyde Navigation, Glasgow
Purchase price £4,360
Arrived 12.1970
Demolition commenced 10.12.1970.

**JAKOB EKKENGA**
Trawler 300/1951
Emder Heringfischerei A.G., Emden
Purchase price £1,400
Arrived 12.1970
Demolition commenced 27.12.1970.

*Portway* at Liverpool. *[J. and M. Clarkson.]*

One which got away, the *Caledonia* of 1934. *[J. and M. Clarkson collection]*

HMS *Trafalgar*. *[Rick Cox collection]*

**LADY OF MANN**
Passenger steamer 3,104/1930
Isle of Man Steam Packet Co. Ltd., Douglas
Arrived c30.12.1971 having sailed from Barrow 29.12.1971
Demolition commenced 10.1.1972.

**BENMACDHUI**
Cargo 7,755/1948
The Ben Line Steamers Ltd., Leith
Arrived 23.4.1972
Demolition commenced 5.6.1972.

**LUGANO**
ex *Hudson Firth* 1967
Cargo 2,925/1949
Compania Naviera Rivabella S.A. (S. Tuillier, Lugano)
Arrived 11.10.1972.
Demolition commenced 15.12.1972.

**CAPABLE**
Tug 832/1946
Royal Navy
Purchase price £20,050
Arrived 5.1973.

**HAFLIDI**
ex *Gardar Thorsteinsson* 1951
Trawler 677/1948
Utgerdarfelag Siglufjardar H/f, Siglufirdi
Purchase price £12,186
Arrived 15.6.1973.

**PLUTO**
Minesweeper 1,010d/1945
Royal Navy
Arrived 10.1973 having been bought 3.9.1972.

**SUCCOUR**
Salvage vessel 775/1944
Royal Navy
Purchase price £20,100
Arrived 11.1973 having been bought 6.9.1973.

**SCARBA**
ex *Scotia* 1972, ex *Fluellen* 1947
Fishery cruiser 492/1940
Secretary of State for Scotland
Purchase price £11,910
Arrived 11.1973.

**OLD LOCHFYNE**
ex *Lochfyne* 1973
Passenger ferry 754/1931
David Macbrayne Ltd., Glasgow
Purchase price £22,000
Arrived 25.3.1974
Demolition commenced 1.4.1974.

**CORK**
ex *Kilkenny* 1971
Coaster 1,320/1937
British and Irish Steam Packet Co. Ltd., Dublin
Arrived 10.6.1974
Demolition commenced 13.6.1974.

*Lady of Mann.* [J. and M. Clarkson]

*Benmacdhui.* [George Gardner collection]

The salvage vessel HMS *Succour*. [J. and M. Clarkson collection]

**MARDINA IMPORTER**
ex *Orica* 1972, ex *Chicanoa* 1970
Refrigerated cargo 6,082/1958
Faith Shipping Co., Monrovia (Maritime
Shipping Agencies Inc., Chicago)
Arrived 23.6.1974
Demolition commenced 6.9.1974.

**RÖDULL**
Trawler 680/1948
Venus H/f, Hafnarfirdi
Arrived 7.10.1974
Later to Troon.

**OMOA**
ex *Changuinola* 1970
Refrigerated cargo 6,079/1957
Empresa Hondurena de Vapores S.A.,
Puerto Limon (United Fruit Co., New York)
Arrived 6.4.1975.

**BRITISH ARCHITECT**
Tanker 22,729/1958
Tanker Charter Co. Ltd., London
Purchase price £297,000
Arrived 29.11.1975
Sale contract dated 3.11.1975
Delivered at London
Demolition commenced 15.12.1975.

**SAMUEL UGELSTAD**
Tanker 2,519/1956
S. Ugelstad, Oslo
Arrived 25.5.1976
Originally of 21,178g the ship had been shortened, converted to diving support ship *Samson Diver* at Gothenburg. Mid section only scrapped commencing 6.1976.

**KAVO PEIRATIS**
ex *Potosi* 1972
Cargo 9,803/1956
Granvias Oceanicas Armadora S.A., Panama (Gourdomichalis Maritime S.A., Piraeus)
Arrived 13.10.1976.
Demolition commenced 22.10.1976.

**PHILINE**
Tanker 30,165/1959
Somerset Shipping Co., Monrovia (Royal Dutch Shell Group, London)
Purchase price £501,600
Contract 2.12.1976
Arrived 19.1.1977.

Two sister-ships arrived within a year of each other, the reefers *Mardina Importer* (top) in June, 1974 and the *Omoa* (above) in April 1975. *[Both: George Gardner collection]*

The *British Architect* (lower middle), which arrived late in 1975, and the *Kavo Peiratis* seen above left at Singapore and right partially demolished in October 1976. *(Lower middle and bottom left: J. and M. Clarkson collection, bottom right: George Gardner collection]*

**SINCERITY**
ex *Kalewa* 1963
Cargo 6,775/1947
Compania de Navegacion Anderson S.A., Panama (S. Tuillier, Lugano)
Arrived 18.5.1977.

**AUTOMEDON**
ex *Cyclops* 1975
Cargo 7,416/1948
Ocean Steam Ship Co. Ltd., Liverpool
Arrived 25.8.1977.

**EMSLAND**
ex *Antonio Zoffi* 1960
Oiler 6,200/1947
West German Navy.
Arrived 31.12.1977.

**FRANKENLAND**
ex *Munsterland* 1959, ex *Powell* 1957
Oiler 11,708/1950
West German Navy
Arrived 4.2.1978.

**EMPIRE ROSA**
Tug 292/1946
Ministry of Defence, London
Demolished by Arnott Young at Luce Bay near Wigtown in early 1978 after breaking moorings 3.12.1977 and beached.

**TORCH**
Lighthouse tender 329/1924
Clyde Port Authority, Glasgow
Arrived 3.1978.

*Sincerity,* the former Henderson *Kalewa.* *[George Gardner collection]*

*Automedon* lying on the outside of the *Sincerity,* awaits her turn. *[George Gardner collection]*

The tanker *Frankenland* in a typical shipbreaking yard setting. *[Ian Johnston]*

**BAY TRADER**
ex *Penny Transoceanic* 1978, ex *Lena* 1974, ex *Tarpenbek* 1970
Cargo 3,917/1954
Contessa Shipping Co.Ltd., Limassol (Naphtec Inspektions und Bereederungs GmbH, Hamburg)
Arrived 13.5.1978
Demolition commenced 1.6.1978.

**GENERAL SIKORSKI**
Cargo 6,785/1957
Polskie Linie Oceaniczne, Gdynia
Arrived 30.5.1978 after damage
Demolition commenced 29.6.1978.

**WIECZOREK**
Ore carrier 1,971/1953
Polska Zegluga Morska, Szczecin
Arrived 11.9.1978.

**JEDNOSC ROBOTNICZA**
Collier 2,003/1950
Polska Zegluga Morska, Szczecin
Arrived 9.10.1978.

**THEOPAES**
ex *Ryuko Maru* 1973, ex *Yamatama Maru* 1969
Tanker 20,621/1960
Vitali Navigation S.A., Panama (S.M. Polemis, London)
Contract 10.10.1978
Arrived 27.10.1978.

**PSTROWSKI**
Collier 1,928/1950
Polska Zegluga Morska, Szczecin
Arrived 20.11.1978.

**CUAO**
ex *Caricuao* 1978, ex *Shell Caricuao* 1976, ex *Gaza* 1960
Tanker 11,225/1954
Maraven S.A., Caracas
Arrived 23.12.1978 in tow from Venezuela.
Resale by Heuvelmann, Holland?

**RAIMA**
ex *Charaima* 1978, ex *Shell Charaima* 1976, ex *Glebula* 1960
Tanker 11,225/1954
Maraven S.A., Caracas
Arrived 23.12.1978 in tow from Venezuela
Resale by Heuvelmann, Holland?

**ELISABETH**
ex *Bowcombe* 1966. Also reported ex *Keynes*
Barge c2,700/1943
Arrived 7.1979
Demolition commenced 1.8.1979.

*Torch* at Dalmuir. Athough she arrived in March 1978 she was still virtually untouched, although sitting on the bottom, in August 1979. *[Ian Johnston]*

The Polish collier *Jednosc Robotnicza*. *[J. and M. Clarkson collection]*

The tanker *Raima* lying alongside her sister-ship *Cuao*. Their careers had been similar and both had been economically renamed for their delivery voyage to Dalmuir. The sunken *Torch* lies in the foreground. *[George Gardner collection]*

**SALLY**
ex *Pinewood* 1967
Barge c2,800/1945
Arrived 7.1979
Demolition commenced
24.8.1979.

**REGAL**
ex *Sakura* 1972, ex *Stolt Sakura* 1972, ex *Stolt Ithaca* 1971, ex *Ithaca Star* 1969, ex *Pajala* 1967
Ore/oil carrier 12,540/1951
Ithaca Star Shipping Ltd., Panama (G. Marcoussis, Piraeus)
Purchase price £294,430
Contract 6.8.1979
Arrived 27.8.1979
Demolition commenced
12.9.1979.

**LATO**
ex *Lommaren* 1971
Cargo 3,880/1952
Lato Shipping Co. S.A., Panama
(N.J. Andriopoulos S.A., Piraeus)
Arrived 4.10.1979.

**DIONYSSOS II**
ex *Caroline* 1975, ex *Ancha* 1967, ex *Alexandra Sartori* 1967
Passenger ferry 2,716/1954
Poros Shipping Co. Ltd., Nicosia
(Vassilios Pavlov, Piraeus)
Arrived 21.11.1979.

**FLOATING CRANE NO.2**
Floating crane c1,600/1908
Formerly owned by Harland and Wolff Ltd., Belfast
Arrived 1980 from Cairnryan.

*Regal* (top) with *Torch* in the foreground still partially submerged. *Lato* (bottom) ran aground about 45 miles off Szczecin, Poland on 11th June 1979. Refloated a week later she was found to be beyond economical repair and sold for breaking up. *[Both: George Gardner]*

## SOURCES AND ACKNOWLEDGEMENTS

We thank all who gave permission for their photographs to be used, and for help in finding photographs we are particularly grateful to Tony Smith, Jim McFaul and David Whiteside of the World Ship Photo Library; to Ian Farquhar, F.W. Hawks, Peter Newall, William Schell, George Scott; and to David Hodge and Bob Todd of the National Maritime Museum, and other museums and institutions listed.

Research sources have included the *Registers* of William Schell and Tony Starke, *Lloyd's Register*, *Lloyd's Confidential Index*, *Lloyd's War Losses*, *Mercantile Navy Lists*, *Marine News* and *Shipbuilding and Shipping Record*. Use of the facilities of the World Ship Society, the Guildhall Library, the National Archives and Lloyd's Register of Shipping and the help of Dr Malcolm Cooper are gratefully acknowledged. Particular thanks also to Heather Fenton for editorial and indexing work, and to Marion Clarkson for accountancy services.

**Moss Hutchison's post-war ships**
Brief histories of the Moss and Hutchison companies appear in 'Sea Breezes' for April 1949 by James Pearce in George Chandler's 'Liverpool Shipping: a Short History' (Phoenix House, London, 1960). The Moss-Lamport connection is explored briefly in Paul Heaton's 'Lamport and Holt Line' (P.M. Heaton, Abergavenny, 2004). Just before the article was completed Nick Robins' 'Birds of the Sea' was published (B. McCall, Portishead, 2007) which includes a chapter on Moss Hutchison. Whilst giving some useful information about the period of General Steam/P&O ownership, this book (which is otherwise very welcome) has little new to say about the early history of Moss or Hutchison and lacks detailed histories of the ships. Geoff Holmes helped with photographs and has contributed very significantly to the second part, scheduled to appear in 'Record' 40. Louis Loughran supplied the artwork for flags and funnels. See also John Cook 'Early Steamship Voyages between Liverpool and the Mediterranean, 1845 - 1849' in John Shepherd, ed., *Sixty Years of the Liverpool Nautical Research Society* (L.N.R.S., Liverpool, 1998) and James Hutchison 'That Drug Danger' (Montrose, 1977, page 48).

**Scottish Shire Line**
The history is largely the work of Ian Farquhar, with the fleet list compiled by Roy Fenton with the help of a partial draft kindly supplied by Bill Harvey, added to by Malcolm Cooper and William Schell, with details checked and exact dates added from the Closed Register files BT108 and BT110 in the National Archives, Kew. The early history of Turnbull has benefited from details in Wray Vamplew's 'Salvesens of Leith' (Scottish Academic Press, Edinburgh, 1975).

**A Fort against the Rising Sun**
The narratives of the two attacks on the *Fort Camosun* are based on the masters' reports, held at the National Archives in files ADM 199/2141 and ADM 199/2146. For general background on the Fort standards see S.C. Heal, 'A Great Fleet of Ships: the Canadian Forts and Parks' (Cordillera Books, Vancouver 1999; reprinted Chatham Publishers, London 2003), and on Japanese Second World War submarine operations see 'Sensuikan! Stories and Battle Histories of the IJN's Submarines' (www.combinedfleet.com/sensuikan.htm).

# SCOTTISH SHIRE LINE: Part 1
## Ian Farquhar

In 1866, James Turnbull told the other shareholders in the ship *Glenclune* (471/1857), of which he was master and part owner, that he wished to sell his shares as he felt the future was in steam. Using his substantial earnings from his voyages in the ship, he set up in business as a shipbroker in Glasgow, taking into partnership Henrik Emil Salvesen. The Turnbull and Salvesen families already had business connections. In 1846 James' brother, George V. Turnbull, had formed a partnership at Leith with Theodor Salvesen, the nephew of Henrik and brother of the better-known Christian. James Turnbull turned to his brother George for help in setting up his business, but George could only persuade the Salvesens to transfer their Glasgow agency business to his brother if a family member, Henrik, was brought into the venture.

Towards the end of 1869, James showed his faith in steam by ordering the *Renfrewshire* from a Port Glasgow shipbuilder. After her completion in 1870, four shares were transferred to Henrik. *Renfrewshire* set a naming pattern that was to last under various ownerships for well over a hundred years, although oddly her name was never repeated. Just possibly this was because of an embarrassing mishap during a trial trip when she was holed whilst carrying invited guests. However, her success in the Mediterranean and Black Sea trades led Turnbull to place a repeat order with Blackwood and Gordon, and in March 1872 *Renfrewshire* was joined by the slightly larger *Lanarkshire*. Initial shareholding was shared between James Turnbull, Henrik Salvesen and Edward Martin, the last-named a young relative of Turnbull who was on the office staff. Within a few years the title Turnbull, Martin and Company was adopted for the shipowning business, as Henrik Salvesen withdrew to set up on his own, acting under the influence of his brother Christian who had never completely trusted James Turnbull.

The first ships were essentially tramps, trading to the Mediterranean and Black Sea ports usually with coal outwards from Britain and returning with grain. Their trading pattern for 1872 (see box) shows *Renfrewshire* making one return voyage from Italy and Spain with what was probably fruit. Each of the ships also loaded in Millwall Dock what may have been general cargo for Greek and Turkish ports. *Renfrewshire* was sold after only three years, leaving *Lanarkshire* trading alone until the slightly larger steamer *Sandringham* was bought in 1874. She was the only second hand acquisition the company ever made, but nevertheless remained in the fleet for 20 years. In 1877 the considerably larger steamer *Ayrshire* joined the fleet, followed by a sister *Buteshire* and the similar *Flintshire*. Two slightly larger ships were built in 1881, *Elginshire* and *Ross-shire*. All continued in general trading, but the fortunes of the firm were to change significantly in 1884.

**Frozen meat from New Zealand**
Following the successful voyage of the Albion Line sailing ship *Dunedin* from Port Chalmers to London between February and May 1882 with the first cargo of frozen meat, New Zealand pastoralists saw great potential in supplying the English market with fresh meat. Up to the time of the pioneering voyage of the *Dunedin* New Zealand sheep farmers only had a market for wool, with old sheep being boiled down for tallow. The sheep population of New Zealand at the time was 13 million. Britain was already importing live animals from other countries to feed a population of 35.6 million in 1882 so there was a ready market for frozen meat once the product had been accepted by consumers.

A number of the larger run holders in New Zealand were wary of the monopoly held by Shaw, Savill of London, the New Zealand Shipping Company of Christchurch, New Zealand and the Albion Line of Glasgow and more so when Shaw, Savill merged with the Glasgow firm in November 1882 to form the Shaw, Savill and Albion Company. The companies had worked closely together from 1874, charging uniform rates and determining which ports would be served. They were happy to send ships to Auckland, Wellington, Lyttelton and Port Chalmers as there were also import cargoes for these population bases, but they were reluctant to call at outports with limited draft and navigation aids as well as inadequate wharf facilities. One such secondary port was Oamaru, just 38 nautical miles north of Port Chalmers. Farmers in the Oamaru catchment area could see it was going to be expensive sending sheep to Port Chalmers for shipment. One of the largest pastoralists in the

**Voyages in 1872**
*Lanarkshire* began her maiden voyage on 9th March when she sailed from the Clyde for Taganrog. Here she loaded a grain cargo for Hull, arriving on 25th May having stopped at Malta, presumably for bunkers. On her second voyage she loaded in Millwall Dock what was presumably general cargo and on 14th June cleared for Smyrna, Constantinople, Galatz and Ibraila. At the last of these, the Danube port now known as Braila, she loaded a cargo of maize which was topped up at Sulina, and then sailed for Falmouth, where she was given orders to proceed to New Ross to discharge, arriving there in late August. On her third voyage she loaded coal at Cardiff for Port Said, and from there once again proceeded to load homeward at the Danube ports, this time calling at Plymouth for orders which took her into the Thames on 17th November.

Meanwhile, the *Renfrewshire* was also trading to the Mediterranean and Danube ports in 1872. At the very beginning of the year she sailed from South Shields for Naples, undoubtedly with coal. The pattern of her return voyage to the Clyde suggests she was loading fruit, as from Naples she called at Messina, Catania, Palermo and Valencia. In March she left Glasgow for Constantinople, and from there was sent to load grain in Ibraila and Sulina. She did not proceed straight to northern Europe, however, but called at Trieste and Barletta before sailing for Dunkirk to discharge. Two further voyages that year saw her load at the Danube ports for, respectively, Marseilles and London. In December 1872 she repeated *Lanarkshire's* voyage from London, clearing Millwall Dock for Piraeus, Smyrna and Constantinople. She then loaded grain in the Danube and came home to Falmouth for orders.

*The officers of the Elderslie at Oamaru, South Island with John Reid seated in the centre. [Ian J. Farquhar collection]*

Oamaru area was John Reid of the Elderslie Estate. Born in Stirling, Scotland in 1835, as a youth he initially migrated to Australia, spending his first ten years as an engineer at Ballarat. In 1863 he came to Otago and started to buy land. He named his main farm Elderslie and, when he took up residence there in 1874, he was grazing around 33,000 sheep. Reid conceived the idea that he and other farmers in the area could generate sufficient stock to justify direct sailings from Oamaru to London. In 1883 he took his wife to Britain for her health and, during their time in Scotland, Reid met with Turnbull, Martin and Company and encouraged the company to build a special ship for the trade, which he would undertake to charter for the first three years. The contract to build a refrigerated ship for the New Zealand trade was a bold move and would clearly provoke retaliation from the other two lines trading to New Zealand.

The ship was built by Palmers, Jarrow and launched as *Elderslie* by Mrs Adamson on 30th April 1884, and she left the Tyne for Oamaru on 28th June, arriving at that port on 24th August. Ownership was registered to the Elderslie Steamship Co. Ltd. She was barque rigged and carried sails for use on the long ocean passages. She also had passenger accommodation for ten passengers in first class, 50 in second class and 150 in third class although in service she invariably carried only a few. The whole of her 'tween decks were insulated with charcoal and she could freeze the cargo to 20 degrees below freezing point. She had a capacity for around 25,000 carcasses of mutton, adequate for the availability of cold storage at London at the time. The average carcass weight was about 32 kgs compared to the 13.5 kg lamb carcasses that British customers preferred in later years. Her propulsion came from a two-cylinder compound inverted engine able to give her a speed of around nine knots. Prior to her arrival special killing facilities were established at Eveline, near the port of Oamaru, and killing began two days before *Elderslie* arrived, with the carcasses then being taken to the ship and frozen on board. John Reid was feted by the people of Oamaru and presented with a large 69.5 oz silver salver at a special reception in his honour. *Elderslie* loaded 23,304 carcasses of mutton, 3,098 sacks of wheat, 74 sacks of turnip seed, 172 bales of wool, 73 bales of skins, a few casks of tallow and sailed for Port Chalmers on 15th October to load sufficient coal bunkers for the passage to London, which took 62 days. The cargo out turned in fine condition and *Elderslie* arrived back in Oamaru for a second cargo on 18th March 1885. John Reid found he was not getting full support from his farmer friends in the area and this time *Elderslie* had to top up at Port Chalmers with 9,200 carcasses. On this voyage 4,000 carcasses were condemned as 'unfit for food' and Reid was concerned at the costs that might fall on him personally if any further problems arose in the future. He was a director of the New Zealand Refrigerating Company which had built the first freezing works in New Zealand at Dunedin in 1881 and he arranged with this company to assume responsibility for the supply of frozen meat for the duration of his contract. The presence of *Elderslie* in the trade had attracted support from other ports. Whilst Oamaru and Port Chalmers were to remain the most frequent ports of loading in the following few years, calls were also made to the South Island ports of Lyttelton, Timaru and Bluff.

The potential for the export of frozen meat from New Zealand saw Turnbull, Martin and Company build further ships for the trade, bringing in *Fifeshire* in 1887, *Nairnshire* in 1889 and *Morayshire* in 1890, all new steamers with refrigerated capacity for around 50,000 carcasses of mutton. Rather than ballast the 12,000 miles to New Zealand, Turnbull, Martin endeavoured to charter the vessels to companies having service rights with the Australian conference for the passage from London to Australia, the vessels then crossing to New Zealand to load. Amongst the lines the ships were chartered to for the outward voyage were Trinder, Anderson's West Australian Steam Navigation Company, Houlder Brothers, and later the British India Associated Lines on the latter's London to Queensland service.

The first Nairnshire at Port Chalmers. *[David de Maus]*

The first Morayshire at Port Chalmers. *[David de Maus]*

Initially freight on frozen meat was 2.25 pence per pound but competition from Tyser and Company saw the rate slip to as low as 1.75 pence per pound at times. Turnbull, Martin did not have the resources, or ships, to mount a fully competitive, regular service as Shaw, Savill and Albion and the New Zealand Shipping Company were able to do, but the Shire vessels certainly developed a permanence in the trade and were a constant source of nuisance to the established lines. *Fifeshire* loaded at Timaru, Oamaru and Port Chalmers on her maiden voyage in January 1888 and *Nairnshire* arrived at Bluff on 18th November 1889. *Morayshire* loaded at Port Chalmers, Lyttelton, Napier and Wellington for London in May 1890. All the ships continued to be registered to the Elderslie Steamship Co. Ltd. and - although retaining their offices at 8 Gordon Street, Glasgow - Turnbull, Martin and Company opened premises at 112 Fenchurch Street, London to better deal with the ship calls at that port and the discharge and delivery of the inward cargoes from New Zealand. In New Zealand the line was advertised as the 'Shire Line of Direct Steamers' until 1911 when the advertisements referred to the 'Shire Line of Steamers'. After the First World War the title used was just the 'Shire Line'. From the early 1890s Turnbull, Martin and Company had its only New Zealand office in Dunedin. It also acted as agents for the New Zealand Shipping Company, and later Federal, and only closed in 1930 after the New Zealand Shipping Company decided to open its own office in Dunedin.

A fourth vessel, *Elginshire*, sailed from London on 11th November 1891 for Adelaide and Sydney but she had a very short life being wrecked at Normanby, south of Timaru on 9th March 1892. She was still on her maiden voyage. She had loaded 12,416 carcasses of mutton at Rockhampton, Queensland and then sailed to Oamaru where she loaded 13,029 carcases. She cleared Oamaru at midnight on the 8th for the 50-mile passage to Timaru. Dense fog was encountered and she stranded five miles south of Timaru on the only danger spot between the two ports. She was due to load 12,000 carcasses of mutton at Timaru, and was then to proceed to Port Chalmers to top-off before departing for London. A portion of the Oamaru cargo was either loaded into small craft able to go alongside or jettisoned. All attempts to pull *Elginshire* into deep water failed and she was abandoned to the underwriters on 14th March. The master lost out at the enquiry and was criticised for not altering course to the east (proceeding out to sea) but although he had to pay the costs of the inquiry he was able to retain his certificate. A further attempt to refloat *Elginshire* was made in September 1892 but she remained firmly aground, the hull eventually breaking in two, with the wreck visible off the beach for many years.

*To be concluded*

*Morayshire* (1) as *Duke of Portland*. In contrast to the *Duke of Norfolk*, owner James Westray has yet to remove her yards from the fore mast. *[Ian J. Farquhar collection]*

# Fleet list, part 1

1. RENFREWSHIRE 1870-1873 Iron
O.N. 65066 818g 506n
200.5 x 28.2 x 13.5 feet
C. 2-cyl. by Blackwood and Gordon, Port Glasgow; 96 NHP.
*21.6.1870:* Launched by Blackwood and Gordon, Port Glasgow (Yard No.104).
*3.7.1870:* Registered in the ownership of James Turnbull, Port Glasgow as RENFREWSHIRE.
*6.1873:* Sold to David Wallace, Glasgow.
*1878:* Sold to William Weir, Glasgow.
*1880:* Sold to H.L. Seligmann and Son, Glasgow.
*1886:* Sold to Bost and Turner (R. MacKill and Co., managers), Glasgow.
*21.11.1891:* Sold to Fravega e Capurro, Genoa, Italy and renamed MONTE CRISTO.
*25.11.1891:* Register closed.
*1893:* Sold to Marini e Brichetto, Genoa and renamed EDEN.
*1896:* Sold to A. Perugia, Genoa.
*1900:* Sold to Péan, Oran and renamed JEAN BAPTISTE.
*1902:* Sold to A. Parodi fu B., Genoa and renamed PINO.
*1907:* Sold to Societa Saline Italiane (Comm. G. Malato, manager), Genoa and renamed SALINE ITALIANE.
*31.3.1908:* Beached at Galliola Point to prevent her foundering whilst on a voyage from Fiume to Trapani with a cargo of timber. Subsequently refloated and broken up at Naples.

2. LANARKSHIRE 1871-1877 Iron
O.N. 65072 929g 597n
210.0 x 28.2 x 21.5 feet
C.2-cyl. by Blackwood and Gordon, Port Glasgow; 96 NHP.
*2.12.1871:* Launched Blackwood and Gordon, Port Glasgow (Yard No. 113).
*7.3.1872:* Registered in the ownership of Edward Turnbull, Emil Salvesen and Andrew Martin, Port Glasgow as LANARKSHIRE.
*1877:* Sold to George Miller Junior, Port Glasgow.
*1877:* Sold to Burrell and Sons, Glasgow.
*15.1.1882:* Wrecked on Codling Bank, off County Wicklow, whilst on a voyage from Glasgow to Lisbon with a cargo of coal.
*6.2.1882:* Register closed.

3. SANDRINGHAM 1874-1894 Iron
O.N. 65439 948g 738n
*1899:* 1,029g 692n
*1905:* 1,114g 692n
230.0 x 30.3 x 19.0 feet
C.2-cyl. by Thomas Richardson and Sons, Hartlepool; 120 NHP.
*27.4.1872:* Launched by Backhouse and Dixon, Middlesbrough (Yard No. 74).
*18.7.1872:* Registered in the ownership of George D. Dale, North Shields as SANDRINGHAM.
*1874:* Sold to F.G. Swan, Glasgow.
*1874:* Acquired by James Turnbull, Glasgow.
*1877:* Transferred to Turnbull, Martin and Co., Glasgow.
*3.11.1894:* Register closed on sale to G.B. e A. Capellino, Genoa, Italy and renamed SORIA.
*1899:* Sold to A. Monge et A. Jauffret, Cette, France, and renamed ALBERT.
*1902:* Transferred to A. Monge, France.
*1905:* Sold to Guttmann and Company, Libau, Russia and renamed CHARLOTTE.
*29.1.1906:* Abandoned 20 miles west of Lonstrup whilst on a voyage from Riga to Grangemouth with a cargo of pitwood.

4. AYRSHIRE (1) 1877-1889 Iron
O.N. 76783 1,331g 871n
260.3 x 32.3 x 22.5 feet
C.2-cyl. by Walker, Henderson and Co., Glasgow; 140 NHP.
*5.1877:* Launched by William Hamilton and Co., Port Glasgow (Yard No. 40).
*27.6.1877:* Registered in the ownership of Turnbull, Martin and Co., Glasgow as AYRSHIRE.
*1889:* Sold to Walter Runciman and Co., South Shields.
*14.11.1897:* Transferred to North Moor Steamships Ltd. (Walter Runciman and Co., managers), Newcastle-upon-Tyne.
*19.11.1901:* Register closed on sale to Navigation à Vapeur Egée (P.M. Courtgi and Co., managers), Constantinople, Turkey and renamed ALEXANDRIA.
*1912:* Sold to Harcoupis, Vernudakis & Co., Piraeus, Greece.
*1914:* Renamed BARLETTA under the Italian flag.
*1915:* Renamed ALEXANDRIA under the Greek flag. Laid up at Constanza.
*12.1915:* Sold to Manizade Haci Ibrahim, Istanbul, as agent of the Turkish Government.
*29.4.1916:* Reported arriving at Varna and subsequently at Istanbul.
*1922:* Deleted from 'Lloyd's Register'.

5. BUTESHIRE (1) 1877-1889 Iron
O.N. 78558 1,332g 872n
260.3 x 32.3 x 22.7 feet
C.2-cyl. by Walker, Henderson and Co., Glasgow; 467 NHP.
*10.1877:* Launched by William Hamilton and Co., Port Glasgow (Yard No. 41).
*26.11.1877:* Registered in the ownership of Turnbull, Martin and Co., Glasgow as BUTESHIRE.
*1889:* Sold to Walter Runciman and Co., South Shields.
*1890:* Transferred to the South Shields Steamship Co. Ltd. (Walter Runciman and Co., managers), South Shields.
*28.4.1897:* Owners became the Moor Line Ltd. (Walter Runciman and Co., managers), South Shields.
*15.11.1897:* Stranded five miles east north east of Havringe, Sweden whilst on a voyage from Swinemunde to Oxelosund in ballast and became a total loss.
*21.12.1897:* Register closed.

6. FIFESHIRE (1) 1878-1883 Iron
O.N. 78602 1,331g 873n
260.0 x 32.3 x 22.6 feet
C.2-cyl. by Walker, Henderson and Co., Glasgow; 467 NHP.
*4.1878:* Launched by William Hamilton and Co., Port Glasgow (Yard No. 42).
*14.5.1878:* Registered in the ownership of Turnbull, Martin and Co., Glasgow as FIFESHIRE.
*28.8.1883:* Wrecked seven to eight miles north of Cabo Roca, Spain whilst on a voyage from Cardiff to Malta with a cargo of coal.
*20.9.1883:* Register closed.

7. ROSS-SHIRE 1881-1890 Iron
O.N. 84320 1,965g 1,362n
285.0 x 36.0 x 22.8 feet
C.2-cyl. by Blair and Co. Ltd., Stockton-on-Tees; 203 NHP.
*30.4.1881:* Launched by Edward Withy and Co., Hartlepool (Yard No. 96).
*14.6.1881:* Registered in the ownership of Turnbull, Martin and Co., Glasgow as ROSS-SHIRE.
*1897:* Sold to W.S. Miller and Co., Glasgow.
*4.1.1899:* Sank following a collision with the French steamer DUGUESCLIN (1,764/1882), which also sank, 17 miles off Trevose Head whilst on a voyage from Cardiff to St. Nazaire with a cargo of coal.
*11.1.1899:* Register closed.

8. ELGINSHIRE (1) 1882-1890 Iron
O.N. 85899 1,951g 1,353n
285.5 x 36.0 x 22.7 feet
C.2-cyl. by Blair and Co. Ltd., Stockton-on-Tees; 203 NHP.
*22.12.1881:* Launched by Edward Withy and Co., Hartlepool (Yard No. 103).
*23.2.1882:* Registered in the ownership of Turnbull, Martin and Co., Glasgow as ELGINSHIRE.
*21.4.1890:* Wrecked on Topaitilla Reef, Vera Cruz whilst on a voyage from Maryport to Vera Cruz with pumps and railway material.
*21.9.1890:* Register closed.

9. ELDERSLIE 1884-1898 Iron
O.N. 89929 2,761g 1,801n
300.0 x 40.0 x 23.9 feet
C.2-cyl. by Palmer's Shipbuilding and Iron Co. Ltd., Newcastle-upon-Tyne; 306 NHP.
*30.4.1884:* Launched by Palmer's Shipbuilding and Iron Co. Ltd., Newcastle-upon-Tyne (Yard No. 538).
*20.6.1884:* Registered in the ownership of Turnbull, Martin and Co., Glasgow as ELDERSLIE.
*12.10.1887:* Transferred to the Elderslie Steamship Co. Ltd. (Turnbull, Martin and Co., managers), Glasgow.
*6.5.1898:* Sold to the Talbot Steamship Co. Ltd. (T. Bowen Rees and Co., managers), London.
*28.3.1899:* Sold to the Simpson Steamship Co. Ltd. (William Simpson, manager), Cardiff.

A pictorial view of Oamaru with the fully-rigged *Elderslie* berthed. *[Ian J. Farquhar collection]*

*1.10.1900:* Renamed ELLAMY.
*1.5.1905:* Wrecked at Tokora, Kitami, Japan whilst on a coastal voyage.
*21.7.1905:* Register closed.

10. FIFESHIRE (2) 1887-1898
O.N. 95010 3,720g 2,425n
345.0 x 47.6 x 24.1 feet.
T.3-cyl. by Blair and Co. Ltd., Stockton-on-Tees; 400 NHP.
*28,.1887:* Launched by C.S. Swan and Hunter Ltd., Wallsend-on-Tyne (Yard No. 105).
*5.10.1887:* Registered in the ownership of the Elderslie Steamship Co. Ltd. (Turnbull, Martin and Co., managers), Glasgow as FIFESHIRE.

*18.6.1898:* Sold to Duke of Fife Steamship Co. Ltd. (James B. Westray and Co., managers), London.
*8.7.1898:* Renamed DUKE OF FIFE.
*6.7.1903:* Sold to William F. Mitchell, London.
*22.10.1903:* Sold to Morioka Makoto, Uraga, Japan, and renamed ITSUKUSHIMA MARU.
*8.12.1903:* British register closed.
*1912:* Sold to M. Ojiro, Kobe, Japan.
*1918:* Sold to Yamashita Kisen K.K., Kobe.
*1921:* Sold to Shimizu Kisen K.K. (Kuhara Shoji K.K.), Higshitomita, Japan
*1924:* Sold to Kuhara Kogyo K.K., Amino, Japan.

*1927:* Sold to Nippon Kosen Gyogyo K.K., Habu, Japan.
*1932:* Transferred to Nippon Godo Kosen K.K., Habu, Japan.
*3.1933:* Demolition began in Japan.

11. NAIRNSHIRE (1) 1889-1898
O.N. 96079 3,720g 2,428n
350.5 x 47.7 x 24.2 feet
T.3-cyl. by R. and W. Hawthorn, Leslie and Co. Ltd., Hebburn-on-Tyne; 306 NHP.
*11.7.1889:* Launched by R. and W. Hawthorn, Leslie and Co. Ltd., Hebburn-on-Tyne (Yard No. 287).
*15.8.1889:* Registered in the ownership of the Elderslie Steamship Co. Ltd. (Turnbull, Martin and Co., managers), Glasgow as NAIRNSHIRE.
*20.7.1898:* Sold to the Duke of Norfolk Steamship Co. Ltd. (James B. Westray and Co., managers), London.
*28.7.1898:* Renamed DUKE OF NORFOLK.
*5.1905:* Sold to C. Andersen, Hamburg, Germany and renamed MARCELLUS.
*13.7.1905:* British register closed.
*10.1908:* Sold to Reederei A/B Banco (C.J. Banck, manager), Stockholm, Sweden and renamed JOHANNA.
*1914:* Sold to Const. Ath. Papageorgacopulo, Patras, Greece, and renamed PERICLES.
*24.5.1914:* Foundered after hitting submerged wreckage 90 miles off Ouessant whilst on a voyage from Swansea to Alexandria with a cargo of coal.

The second *Fifeshire*. *[David de Maus]*

*Nairnshire* (1) (upper) carrying a full set of yards and as *Duke of Norfolk* (lower). *[Both: Ian J. Farquhar collection]*

**12. MORAYSHIRE (1) 1890-1898**
O.N. 97607  3,822g 2,481n
350.5 x 47.7 x 24.1 feet
T.3-cyl. by R. and W. Hawthorn, Leslie and Co. Ltd., Hebburn-on-Tyne; 300 NHP, 2,000 IHP, 11 knots.
*9.12.1889:* Launched by R. and W. Hawthorn, Leslie and Co. Ltd., Hebburn-on-Tyne (Yard No. 293).
*22.2.1890:* Registered in the ownership of the Elderslie Steamship Co. Ltd. (Turnbull, Martin and Company, managers), Glasgow as MORAYSHIRE.
*8.4.1898:* Sold to James B. Westray, London.
*25.4.1898:* Transferred to the Duke of Portland Steamship Co. Ltd. (James B. Westray and Co., managers), London.
*28.4.1898:* Renamed DUKE OF PORTLAND.
*3.5.1905:* Sold to Nelson Line (Liverpool) Ltd. (H. and W. Nelson Ltd., managers), London.
*7.6.1905:* Renamed HIGHLAND FLING.
*7.1.1907:* Stranded in Kennack Bay, Cornwall during a voyage from London and Falmouth to Cardiff.
*20.1.1907:* After part towed to Falmouth and subsequently demolished.
*11.4.1907:* Register closed.

**13. ELGINSHIRE (2) 1891-1892**
O.N. 98671  4,579g 2,980n
364.0 x 48.1 x 25.0 feet
T. 3-cyl. by the Wallsend Slipway Co. Ltd., Wallsend-on-Tyne; 450 NHP, 2,400 IHP, 11.5 knots.
*2.9.1891:* Launched by C. S. Swan and Hunter, Wallsend-on-Tyne (Yard No. 167).
*2.10.1891:* Registered in the ownership of the Elderslie Steamship Co. Ltd. (Turnbull, Martin and Co., managers), Glasgow as ELGINSHIRE.
*9.3.1892:* Wrecked 200 yards off Normanby Point, four miles south of Timaru, New Zealand whilst on coastal passage from Oamaru to Timaru to continue loading during a voyage from Rockhampton to London with a cargo of meat and wool.
*9.11.1892:* Register closed.

*Morayshire* (1) (above) and as the *Highland Fling* (right) aground in Kennack Bay during January 1907. *[Above: Ian J. Farquhar collection, right: J. and M. Clarkson collection]*

The conclusion of the maiden voyage of the second *Elginshire* (below), wrecked off Timaru, South Island. *[Ian J. Farquhar collection]*

# OVERSEAS FRUIT SHIPS IN HOBART 1960-1976: Part 1

## Rex Cox

Captain William Bligh is credited with introducing apples to Tasmania in 1792, when a botanist aboard HMS *Bounty* planted the first trees at Adventure Bay, Bruny Island. While the first commercial consignment was despatched to England early in the 19th century, and there are records of further small shipments in 1849 and 1851, Tasmania did not become a major exporter until the 1880s. A supervised shipment of 100 cases to Britain in 1884 arrived in such good condition that growers were encouraged to further develop the trade, while the introduction of on-board refrigeration really put the industry on its feet. By the early 20th century ships of P&O, Orient, Aberdeen, Scottish Shire and Federal were regularly loading apples and pears in Hobart between February and April. In 1907, 400,000 cases were shipped, with Federal Line's *Durham* (5,561/1904) taking the first large consignment of 125,000 cases.

The Huon Valley became the focal point for fruit growing in the south of the island, its products being shipped not only from the Hobart wharves but also through the outports of Port Huon and Cygnet. Similarly, the Tamar Valley was the main orchard area in the north of the state, exporting from the wharves at Beauty Point and Inspection Head on the lower reaches of the Tamar River, near Launceston.

Initially, the overseas trade was exclusively with the United Kingdom, but markets were gradually developed elsewhere, particularly in Scandinavia and Germany, and later in South East Asia. Important domestic outlets were also created in other Australian states, with weekly shipments by coastal cargo vessels to Melbourne and Sydney, less frequently to Brisbane. Tasmania became known as 'the Apple Isle', so important was this industry to the local economy.

British cargo liners from the conference lines dominated the export trade for many years, though the introduction in the mid-1950s of small, fast refrigerated vessels by Sweden's Transatlantic Line pointed to future developments. Another Swedish company, Salén Line, began lifting fruit from Hobart in 1964, and by the end of the decade their owned and chartered reefers were handling most of the cargoes.

In 1961 – a fairly typical year – more than fifty ships loaded fruit at Hobart and Port Huon for UK and Continental ports, Scandinavia and South East Asia. Some 80 per cent of these ships were British, belonging to Blue Funnel, British India, China Navigation, Eastern and Australian, Blue Star, Port, Federal-New Zealand Shipping, Shaw Savill, Clan, and P&O. Swedish, Norwegian and Dutch vessels of Transatlantic, Wilhelmsen and Royal Interocean Lines made up the balance.

The industry peaked in 1964, with nearly six million cases of fruit shipped to overseas and interstate destinations. Then began a steady decline, hastened by drought, bushfires and the loss of traditional markets.

From the late 1960s, some ships owned by Far Eastern interests handled cargoes for Hong Kong, Singapore and Manila. Though often in the twilight of their careers, they looked attractive and well maintained and provided a contrast to the better-known British and European cargo liners.

Decline accelerated during the 1970s, resulting in only ten ships loading in 1980. Ten years later that number was down to four and the final shipment left Hobart in August 1995. While there were experiments with direct container shipments, most cargoes in later years were lifted by relatively small Japanese-built reefers. Nowadays, all Tasmanian fruit exports are containerised and shipped via Melbourne.

Fortunately, the Hobart Branch of the World Ship Society boasted a number of keen photographers during the period that the fruit trade was at its post-war peak. These particular photographs are the work of the late Noel Brown and Kingsley Barr, and through their generosity now form part of my own collection.

---

**IMPERIAL STAR** (opposite top)
*Harland and Wolff Ltd., Glasgow, 1948; 13,181gt, 572 feet.*
*Two 8-cyl. 2SCDA oil engines by Harland and Wolff Ltd., Glasgow.*
Unlike some ships in the Vestey empire, *Imperial Star* led a fairly uncomplicated life. Completed for Union Cold Storage Co. Ltd., with Blue Star as managers, the only significant change was restyling of her owners in 1949 as Union International Co. Ltd. She inherited the handsome profile of a series of pre-war Blue Star liners which had commenced with her 1935 namesake, a Malta convoy casualty in September 1941.

The second *Imperial Star* visited Hobart six times and was looking distinctly shabby when photographed on 9th March 1966, prior to loading fruit at Port Huon for Antwerp, Hamburg, Hull and London. She arrived at the (then) inevitable Kaohsiung shipbreakers' yard on 17th September 1971 – one of many victims of containerisation in the first half of the 1970s.

**NEWCASTLE STAR** (below)
*Bremer Vulkan, Vegesack, 1956;
8,398gt, 519 feet.
10-cyl. 2SCSA M.A.N.-type oil engine
by Bremer Vulkan, Vegesack.*
Blue Star Line raised a few eyebrows when it placed orders in West Germany for this vessel, her sisters *Canberra Star* and *Hobart Star*, and the larger *Gladstone Star* and *Townsville Star* (both 10,725/1957). While the others were initially registered in Hamilton, Bermuda, and the ownership of Salient Shipping Co. (Bermuda) Ltd., *Newcastle Star* had London on her stern. She is pictured arriving at the Hobart wharves in 1961, framed by two Australian coastal freighters owned by Union Steam Ship Co. of New Zealand Ltd.

Renamed *Montevideo Star* on transfer to the South American service in 1973, she then went to the Cypriot flag as *Golden Madonna* in 1976, with a transfer to Greek registry two years later. Her career ended with her arrival at Kaohsiung on 13th March 1980.

## AMERICA STAR
*Bartram and Sons Ltd., Sunderland, 1964; 7,899gt, 463 feet.*
*8-cyl. 2SCSA Sulzer-type oil engine by George Clark Ltd., Sunderland.*

Almost brand new when photographed on her first Hobart arrival, 15th April 1965, *America Star* took fruit for Rotterdam, Oslo and London. Nearby, *Port Sydney* (9,992/1955) was discharging general cargo from the UK.

*America Star* was lengthened in 1973 by Framnaes, Sandefjord, along with *Halifax Star* and *New York Star*. An extra 78 feet increased her tonnage to 9,253 gross. She was renamed *Golden Princess* in 1982 for Vermerar Compania Naviera S.A., Panama (Kappa Maritime Ltd.) and broken up at Shanghai in 1984.

## RENOIR
*William Pickersgill and Sons Ltd., Sunderland, 1953; 4,300gt, 411 feet.*
*6-cyl. 4 SCSA oil engine by Harland and Wolff Ltd., Glasgow.*

Putting out copious amounts of smoke while berthing at Port Huon on 23rd May 1970, *Renoir* was no stranger to southern Tasmania. She had been here many times as *Malay* and later as *Mahsuri* for Austasia Line, whose funnel colours she still carried when this photo was taken.

Her history provides a sort of 'Who's Who' of the Vestey Group. Originally ordered by the Booth Line as *Clement*, she was launched on 4th October 1952 as *Malay Star* for Blue Star Line. During fitting out she transferred to the newly-formed Austasia Line and had the Star suffix dropped from her name. Following Austasia's introduction in 1964 of the passenger/cargo vessel *Malaysia* (8,062/1955, formerly *Hubert* of Booth Line), *Malay* was renamed *Mahsuri* to avoid confusion. In 1966 she went in the other direction to Booth Line as *Benedict*, and the following year adopted the Lamport and Holt name *Renoir* though still registered in Booth's ownership. Booth sold her in 1971 to Starlight Steamship Company S.A., Panama, and she became *Diamond Star*. She was sold to breakers in Taiwan, and left Kaohsiung for Suao on 12th October 1973.

## CLAN MACDONALD
*Greenock Dockyard Co. Ltd., Greenock, 1939; 8,141gt, 505 feet.*
*Two 10-cyl. 4SCSA Burmeister & Wain-type oil engines by J.G. Kincaid and Co. Ltd., Greenock.*

Clan Macdonald made no less than 13 visits to Hobart in 18 years, not always for fruit – though she became something of a regular in that trade, calling every season from 1957 to 1964 and for the last time in 1966, when this photograph was taken. She is shown approaching her berth on 16th May, to load for London, Liverpool and Glasgow. Wilhelmsen's *Talabot* (6,104/1946) can be seen to the right, taking hides and skins for Continental ports.

While assisting *Clan Macdonald* at Beauty Point on 15th May 1968, the tug *Wybia* (217/1967) collided with the cargo liner's propeller and was holed in four places. Beached on a nearby sandbank, *Wybia* was refloated on 24th May and towed to Launceston for docking and repairs.

*Clan Macdonald* had survived Malta convoys during the Second World War and in fact lasted a creditable 31 years, arriving at Shanghai for scrapping on 6th August 1970. For the last ten years of her life she was registered in the ownership of Houston Line Ltd.

## AYRSHIRE
*Greenock Dockyard Co. Ltd., Greenock, 1957; 9,360gt, 535 feet.*
*Three steam turbines double-reduction geared to a single screw, by Parsons Marine Steam Turbine Co. Ltd., Wallsend-on-Tyne.*

Visually announcing her departure from Hobart on 16th March 1962, *Ayrshire* was the last Clan liner completed with a Scottish Shire name. She and her sister *Argyllshire* (9,299/1956) represented the final development of a group of 12 cargo liners built by the Greenock Dockyard Co. Ltd. for Clan Line and Pacific Steam Navigation Company Ltd. (together with another built for the latter company by Denny at Dumbarton). With accommodation for 12 passengers, these vessels were noted for their handsome lines and distinctive smoke-deflecting funnels.

The two Shires were somewhat larger than the rest, with number one hatch situated on an extended forecastle and an extra (sixth) hold aft. A bipod mainmast was another distinguishing feature, while in common with many Clan liners they were well equipped for heavy lifts – two 40-ton derricks and one of 105 tons. Four of their six holds were refrigerated, and both loaded fruit at Hobart in 1958, then became familiar visitors in the sixties. *Ayrshire* called another four times before her unfortunate demise, and *Argyllshire* six times.

*Ayrshire* went aground on 23rd March 1965 at Abd-al-Kuri, near the mouth of the Gulf of Aden, while on a voyage from Liverpool to Brisbane. She was refloated on 26th April but was almost immediately swept aground again by strong currents, and ended up broadside to the shore. Salvage operations were then abandoned. The story is told in detail in 'Clan Line: Illustrated Fleet History'.

## PORT HOBART
*Harland and Wolff Ltd., Belfast, 1946; 11,149gt, 540 feet.*
*Two 8-cyl. 2SCDA oil engines by Harland and Wolff Ltd., Glasgow.*

The second *Port Hobart* was launched for the Ministry of War Transport as *Empire Wessex*, and subsequently sold to Port Line Ltd. The first of the name (7,448/1925) was one of their early motor ships and a war loss in 1940.

*Port Hobart* was originally fitted with accommodation for over 100 saloon and tourist class passengers, giving her a tonnage when built of 11,861 gross but this was reduced to the statutory 12 passengers in 1950. She was broken up at Shanghai in 1970.

The photographer was up early on 4th May 1963 to capture one of her many arrivals in her name port.

## PORT WELLINGTON
*John Brown and Co. Ltd., Clydebank, 1946; 10,588gt, 529 feet.*
*Two 5-cyl. 2SCSA Doxford-type oil engines by John Brown and Co. Ltd., Clydebank.*

The first *Port Wellington* (8,301/1924) was sunk by the German auxiliary cruiser *Pinguin* (7,862/1936) in December 1940. The second was part of Port Line's postwar rebuilding programme, along with sister ship *Port Pirie* (10,535/1947), a product of Swan, Hunter and Wigham Richardson, who also built the similar *Port Napier* (11,834/1947).

Like all the company's vessels, they were very well known in this part of the world. They not only helped to lift the annual apple and pear crop but maintained a monthly general cargo service from UK ports, with occasional sailings to and from the Continent and USA as well. This happy situation changed abruptly when the Australian trades were containerised in 1969 and 1970 and familiar ships began disappearing from the scene, with *Port Wellington* going to Spanish shipbreakers in 1971.

The photograph was taken in 1963 from an excellent vantage point atop a Marine Board pile driver (try doing that these days!) as *Port Wellington* entered the port of Hobart.

### DURANGO
*Harland and Wolff Ltd., Belfast, 1944; 9,801gt, 469 feet.*
*Two 6-cyl. 2SCDA Burmeister & Wain-type oil engines by Harland and Wolff Ltd., Belfast.*

Arriving on 16th March 1965 – her only Hobart visit – this Royal Mail liner was on a Shaw, Savill charter to load fruit for Avonmouth, Dublin and Liverpool. Deliveries were very slow that season, resulting in a stay of over three weeks, whereas average loading time in the 1960s was ten days. Yet another Port liner discharging general cargo features here – *Port Launceston* (8,957/1957).

Durango's sister ship *Drina* (9,785/1944) and the similar *Deseado* (9,641/1942) and *Darro* (9,732/43) were also seen in Hobart at various times.

Durango was renamed *Ruthenic* when transferred to Shaw, Savill in 1966, then was sold to Embajada Compania Naviera S.A., Panama (Rethymnis and Kulukundis Ltd.) in 1967 as *Sussex* for delivery to Kaohsiung where she was broken up during the following year.

### CYMRIC
*Harland and Wolff Ltd., Belfast, 1953; 11,182gt, 512 feet.*
*Two 6-cyl. 2SCSA Burmeister & Wain-type oil engines by Harland and Wolff Ltd., Belfast.*

Overcast conditions greeted Cymric as she approached her Hobart berth on 28th April 1962. The second of five C-class vessels completed for Shaw, Savill between 1952 and 1957, she was renamed *Durango* in 1973 for Royal Mail's South American service and broken up in 1975.

## ZEALANDIC
*Alexander Stephen and Sons Ltd., Glasgow, 1965; 7,946gt, 481 feet. 8-cyl. 2SCSA Sulzer-type oil engine by Alexander Stephen and Sons Ltd., Glasgow.*

The morning of 25th April 1965 saw Shaw, Savill's *Zealandic* coming up the Derwent on her maiden voyage (having been completed the previous month), to load for London, Belfast and Liverpool. She was back again two years later, while sister ship *Laurentic* (7,964/1965) also called here during the 1973 season.

*Zealandic* went to the Greek flag in 1980 as *Port Launay*, was renamed *Khalij Crystal* for Liberian owners the following year and broken up in 1984.

Her relatively short career with Shaw, Savill reflected the huge changes affecting British ship owners during that period. When she came out her owner's fleet numbered some 32 vessels, but by the end of 1980 all these had gone and only two newer ships remained.

## ADEN
*Alexander Stephen and Sons Ltd., Glasgow, 1946; 9,943gt, 495 feet. Three steam turbines double-reduction geared to a single screw by Alexander Stephen and Sons Ltd., Glasgow.*

*Aden* had been completed as *Somerset* for Federal Steam Navigation Co., but adopted P&O colours and a new name in 1954. *Devon* (9,940/1946) was a sister ship, while New Zealand Shipping Company's *Papanui* (10,002/1943), *Pipiriki* (10,057/1944) and *Paparoa* (10,005/1944) were built to a similar design. All were occasional visitors to Hobart over 20 years.

*Aden* was one of three P&O cargo liners - *Perim* (9,550/1945) and *Patonga* (10,071/1953) being the others - that regularly loaded fruit in Hobart during the 1960s. She was photographed in idyllic conditions from Hobart's Tasman Bridge during her seventh and last visit in 1967. Her final voyage was to Kaohsiung later that year, arriving 8th October.

## NORTHUMBERLAND
*John Brown and Co. Ltd., Clydebank, 1955; 10,335gt, 499 feet.*
*Two 10-cyl. 2SCSA oil engines with single reduction gearing and electro-magnetic slip couplings to a screw shaft by John Brown and Co. Ltd., Clydebank.*
Ordered as *Turakina* for New Zealand Shipping Company but completed for Federal Line, she is seen here on 9th March 1965 when berthing in Hobart to load apples and pears for Hamburg and Hull.

    *Northumberland* ran aground in Grand Harbour, Valletta, on 7th March 1970, but was refloated without damage. She was sold to a Panamanian company in 1972, though registered at Piraeus as *Kavo Astrapi*.

Renamed *Golden City* in 1973 for Guan Guan Shipping (Private) Ltd., Singapore, she went to Hong Kong breakers five years later.

## TONGARIRO
*Bartram and Sons Ltd., Sunderland, 1967; 8,233gt, 526 feet.*
*8-cyl. 2SCSA oil engine by George Clark and North eastern Marine Ltd., Sunderland.*
*Tongariro* completed a quartet of *Taupo*-class cargo liners for New Zealand Shipping Company and Federal, all of which became well known in Hobart over the next decade. They were of considerable interest at the time, being fitted with Hallen derricks on bipod masts and introducing a new colour scheme - light green hull with a dark green band at water line level, topped by the attractive Federal funnel. By the time this photo was taken in May 1976, however, they had been absorbed into P&O's General Cargo Division and were wearing a biscuit-coloured hull and a much criticised blue funnel with white P&O logo.

    On the right is *Gladstone Star*, also loading fruit. Though it was not appreciated at the time, she would be the last Blue Star liner to handle cargo in Hobart.

    *Tongariro* was sold to Greek interests in 1979 as *Reefer Princess*. Renamed *Capetan Leonidas* in 1982, she was laid up at Piraeus the following year and ended her days at Gadani Beach in 1985.

*To be continued*

# AN OLD GLEN
## Richard Cornish

The excellent publication 'Glen and Shire Lines' took me back in time. In no way could I consider myself having been a 'Glen boat man' but the book certainly produced some recollections of the few occasions I did coastal voyages or stood by in King George V Dock under the eagle eye of Mr Cassidy, the resident Superintendent Engineer.

In particular I was thinking of the month or so spent in *Dardanus* (ex *Glenapp*) over 50 years ago, the photos on pages 164 to 167 having triggered these memories. Some might be a bit hazy but there is my old log/diary to at least confirm ports and dates. In late December 1952 I was home on leave from a Far East voyage in *Aeneas* with every anticipation of having the festive season at home. It was not to be as I was summoned to Liverpool, promoted to fourth engineer and despatched to join *Dardanus* in Hull on 23rd December. The whole ship was a shock to the system. The layout, the cabins and public rooms and not least of all the engine room could not have been more different from what I had experienced. I had worked in many ships when serving my apprenticeship but nothing quite like an old Glen. For example, the saloon boasted a piano (I learned later that the famous fast ones did as well), had illuminated signs indicating ladies and gents toilets and a staircase into the saloon from the old passenger deck above. My cabin was spacious compared to a Blue Funnel 'A' class but spartan in comparison, with the cold water-only hinged commode. Lukewarm water was supplied each morning by a Chinese steward of similar vintage to the ship.

I made a very early acquaintance with the Cochrane donkey boiler as the third mate demanded my attention before I had hardly put my bag down. The ship had two deep tanks of palm oil to be discharged in that port before Christmas. More steam was needed so the boiler was to be flashed up forthwith as demonstrated by a home-going junior engineer. I had worked on similar-sized boilers but they had been coal-fired - this was oil-fired but primitive. Flashing-up involved putting on an asbestos gauntlet, picking up a lump of kerosene-soaked waste, opening the oval door above the burner, lighting the waste and dropping it over the end of the burner and slamming the door shut. Next, position yourself like a 100-metre sprinter by the fuel lever, flip it on and rapidly take off up two steps and along the bottom platform the same instant. The boiler blew back every time. Despite that, all went well and the palm oil when brought up to temperature was discharged on schedule.

The machinery consisted of twin eight-cylinder four-stroke engines and three three-cylinder four-stroke diesel generators. When built all these had operated on the air-blast injection system. Diesel oil was injected by compressed air at a pressure up to 1,000 psi. This pressure was necessary to overcome the compression pressure created by the piston in the combustion space. About ten years after these engines were built research had produced a better method known as direct or solid injection. The four ships still had blast injection when transferred to Blue Funnel in 1949 so work was put in hand to convert them to solid injection. Alfred Holt's Superintendent Engineer A.G. Arnold had adopted a very successful system that gave excellent results on the main engines but not so on the diesel generators. The latter were difficult to start quickly with one engineer and frequently had problems with sticking fuel accumulators. These latter sometimes needed an engineer to climb on top of the half-running generator and stand on the offending device to encourage it to operate properly. This practice would give a health and safety person apoplexy today.

The three generator-driven air compressors had their output reduced to 350 psi (air starting pressure for main engines and diesel generators) by removal of the third-stage piston and after-cooler. The huge manoeuvring air compressor (known by a rather vulgar nickname from the noises produced as it gathered speed) was given a similar modification. A version of this fuel system was fitted to some of the Mark III 'A' class and in general proved very successful. The fuel metering pumps were almost identical to those fitted to the old Glens. However, the Mark IIIs ran on heavy fuel and that did cause the gas pumps to stick at the most inopportune moments: for instance, a cylinder or two might cut out in the middle of coming alongside. This was mostly eradicated by injections of gunk or the judicious use of a copper or lead hammer.

To revert to the old Glens, everything was different - the steering gear control from the bridge operated on the Ward-Leonard system, and there were McFarlane winches which as I recollect operated from a single motor but required two drivers working a system of clutches and reverse gears (a supply of grease, lubricating oil and sand had to be within reach of the operator). It used to be said the Australian wharfies would go on strike as soon as one of these ships arrived. The derricks were of the box girder type - one could walk along them if sufficiently foolhardy. My memory is hazy but I am almost sure *Dardanus* had three whistles, if not something different to others of the class and they took more air for one blast than was used to start a main engine. Certainly when in fog or with the engines on stand-by all three generators needed to be on the board so that the big compressor could be in service.

**The flying Chinaman**
The less said about Christmas in Hull the better: in the seafarers' world it wasn't the most exciting port. To add insult to injury we sailed on New Year's Eve for Rotterdam and berthed in the Merwehaven. I have to say Rotterdam had more to offer than Hull. This was followed by a call at the Royal Albert Docks, London for more discharging and we departed there on 9th January bound for Avonmouth. The following night gave rise to the incident that produced the flying Chinaman story. The weather was calm and watch uneventful. At one bell (23.45) the junior engineer asked if he could call the 12-to-4 watch and number 4 greaser to call the reliefs for himself and the topside greaser. The latter announced he would make some tea for the new watch. That left me on my own, so I entered the fuel consumption and engine revs in the log and was just looking forward to a beer before turning in when, without any warning, both telegraphs rang 'stand-by immediately'

followed by 'stop' and finally 'half astern'. I hastened to answer the telegraphs and pull the engine control levers back to the 'stop' position. With the weigh still on the ship the engines of course continued to rotate. I waited as it was not practice to put the reversing gear over until the engines had come to rest (unlike a steam reciprocating engine when reversal can be achieved safely before the engine actually stops). Just then I heard a voice shouting over the machinery noises. It was the Chief Engineer, Mr Gellatley, shouting 'put the gear over'. This was done immediately with the most spectacular results. The ingenious hydraulic reversing gear operates a lay shaft that lifts all the rollers from the camshaft allowing the latter to move into the astern position.

To say the results were spectacular is a gross understatement because in about 20 seconds the Battle of Trafalgar commenced. With the engines still rotating at about fifty or sixty rpm and every valve on every cylinder effectively shut something had to give - the relief valves on every cylinder lifted in sequence with a load report akin to firing a 12-pounder gun and simultaneously releasing a sheet of flame and a great gout of dense black smoke. Within a very short time the engineers and greasers were down below, the stand-by generator was started followed by the big air compressor, and coolers were adjusted. The bridge informed us that we had run into a fog bank but all was clear again. Details were entered in the log, the chief departed and the 8-to-12 handed over to the 12-to-4 watch and we were about to depart for our beer. The third said 'where's the tea?' and I said 'where's our topside greaser?' It transpired almost everyone was on the ladder clearly visible in the centre of the top photo on page 167 in the book when the first relief valve lifted. It was said the 8-to-12 topside greaser had actually reached the top platform when the first valve lifted (one is just visible on the photo – number five starboard cylinder head just opposite the foot of the ladder behind the push rods on the right of the photo). The flame and smoke came out at ankle height. We searched the engine room thinking he was perhaps somewhere injured but could not find him. The greaser was sent to look for him. He returned with the tea box which he found in the working alleyway and said the greaser was in his bunk OK but talking 'allee same mun ji' (crazy man). The matter was discussed a bit longer when we realised that apart from the greaser with the tea box no less than six persons were coming down that ladder as the first relief valve lifted. Everybody turned around and started back up until the smoke cleared, nobody was aware of anyone else pushing past them on the ladder. In no time the myth of the flying Chinaman came into being.

However it did not last long. The following night when anchored off the Scarweather Light (Swansea Bay - more fog) I came up behind the Third Engineer and there on the right shoulder of his boiler suit was a light but distinct oily footprint. A quick check found another on a junior's boiler suit so ending the silly myth of the flying Chinaman. The two greasers were wearing dark blue boiler suits and the Chief his reefer jacket so no marks on them. Nevertheless it is still a mystery as to how the 8-to-12 topside greaser got up that steep ladder over six men and carrying a box with a pot of hot tea without them being aware - fear must have lent him wings!

As a footnote, after Avonmouth we went to Swansea to complete discharge and then proceeded to the Holy Loch. There we paid off and with the aid of two Steel and Bennie's big tugs the ship was laid up on two anchors and a swivel shackle. I was taken to Greenock in the *Wrestler* and eventually caught the overnight train to Liverpool to stand by a ship in Gladstone Dock. It was early morning of 26th January 1953 and what did I see from the Overhead Railway - the *Empress of Canada* lying on her side not long having capsized - Gladstone station was closed and I had to get off at Seaforth to find my ship - and I did not have a camera with me!

Built and engined by Harland and Wolfe Ltd., Glasgow in 1920, *Glenapp* was transferred to Ocean Steam Ship Co. Ltd. and renamed *Dardanus* in January 1949. She was broken up at Inverkeithing in 1957. *[Tom Rayner/J. and M. Clarkson]*

# CLAN LINE FOLLOW UP

Following the publication of our Clan Line history (which, with all due modesty, we have to say has been very well received), we take this opportunity to cover an interesting loose end, and provide additional information and a few corrections.

**The tartan jack**
Some years ago one of the editors had heard from flags and funnels specialist Louis Loughran that Clan Line ships had individual stem jacks supplied which featured the tartan of the Clan after which the ship was named and these were flown when the ship was moored. Although both very familiar with Clan Line ships from many visits to Birkenhead and Liverpool from 1960 onwards, neither of us had seen such a stem jack used, and with firm evidence lacking the practice was not referred to in the Clan Line book. Recently, Harry Hignett came across a Clan Line house flag with the red replaced by a tartan. It was obviously one of these stem jacks, but which? This was not a straightforward question, as each clan had several tartans, including day tartans and dress tartans, which were often very different, but one of Harry's correspondents has identified it as the Mackenzie tartan.

The whole question of flying such jacks was then posed to David Oakden, who has a network of contacts who served with Clan Line. David confirmed that such tartan stem jacks were indeed issued, and the consensus amongst his contacts was that they were introduced after the Second World War, perhaps even in the early 1950s. One informant suggested that the practice was discontinued with the formation of British and Commonwealth in late 1955, after which ships flew a scaled-down version of the house flag of their subsidiary company as a stem jack. Others believe the issue of tartan stem jack ceased as late as 1967, because of the cost and inability to standardise the practice. The latter date is more likely as there is evidence that the 1962-built *Clan Farquharson* was supplied with a tartan flag. It seems that not all ships had a tartan issued (*Clan Cameron* is quoted as such an exception), and that not all masters and mates followed the practice of flying them. Certainly the photographs in our book show that a variety of stem jacks were flown when ships were launched. Thanks to David Oakden, Chris Abbott, C.R. Kelso, Iain Maciver and Sam Davidson for their help with this conundrum.

**Putting out more flags**
David Wittridge and others steeped in flag lore have made a number of points. Firstly, to show she was adjusting compasses, *Manchester Regiment* (page 106) would have flown the flags 'JI' not 'JT'. The 'JI' hoist can be seen in the photograph of *Scottish Ptarmigan* on page 233. David points out that flags flown by *Scottish Hawk* in the photograph on page 339 confirm that she was undergoing speed trials and had a pilot on board, but he notes that she was in fully loaded condition. He also observes that the on page 197 the photographs of *Royal Star* and *Caledonian Star* have been transposed.

John Woodley notes that in the photograph of *Clan Stewart* on page 258 the international code flags denoting that she is running trials are not displayed and he suggests that she has completed trials, has returned to port, loaded and departed on her first voyage. Looking at the increased turbulence at the propeller he thinks she has just dropped off the pilot and has rung for increased speed.

**Indian Queens**
Malcolm Cooper corrects the statement on page 16 that Queen Line withdrew from its Indian service in early 1882. In fact the Queen Steamship Co. Ltd. went into liquidation in 1879, and its remaining ships were lost or sold in 1880. Malcolm adds that Cayzer would have known all about the Queen Line, as some of its shares were held by Cayzer's backer, John Muir.

*King Alfred*: **fact or fiction?**
Malcolm Whiteley comments on the black funnel of the bulk carrier *King Alfred* in the upper photograph on page 312. He reckons this is a trials photograph, and her pristine condition seems to confirm this, but if so she would carry the name *Angelus* and the funnel of owners Olsen and Ugelstads with interlinked letters O and U in white on black. Could it be that a photograph of *Angelus* on trials was retouched to change her name and obliterate the original funnel colours?

**What, no Stülckens?**
A.D. Frost makes an interesting point. When they were so keen to carry heavy lifts, why did such a progressive company as Clan Line stick to old-fashioned jumbo derricks and not adopt the more modern Stülcken mast? Competitors such as Harrison Line, Blue Star, British India and Scindia certainly did so. He was once told by a Clan Line mate that a royalty had to be paid to Stülckens every time a heavy list was made, but this sounds apocryphal. He also wonders whether Norwegian heavy lifters Christen Smith lost out to Hansa Line because they rejected the Stülcken mast.

**Additions and amendments**
Markus Berger adds that after the sale of *Clan Forbes* (4) and renaming *Arya Man* she was from 31st December 1970 to 24th August 1973 in the ownership of K.G. Taspa Schiffahrts GmbH & Co. (Unimar Seetransport GmbH, managers) of Lübeck, where she was registered. It turns out that Markus took the photograph of *Zhe Hai 3*, the former *Clan Sutherland*, which appears on page 257. He reports himself very pleased that at the exact time she passed his ship the armed Red Guard stationed outside his cabin decided to step away briefly, allowing him to use his camera. Incidentally, in a late correction to the text on page 256 which could not be checked before printing, her name was incorrectly spelt *Zhe Hat 3*. Bob Todd thinks the name would be *Zhan Dou 3*, but a knowledge of mandarin is needed to confirm this!

Bob Todd notes that *Clan Lamont* (3) on pages 158 and *Clan Chattan* on page 181 are carrying Chipchase rafts, and not Carley floats. He also corrects a number of dates: *Clan Macintosh* (page 76) was attacked by *UC 71* on 5.7.1917; *Clan Chattan* (3) (page 181) was launched on 9.3.1944; the year of the grounding of *Ayrshire* (2) (page 271) was 1965. Bob also notes that the details for *Warwick Castle* which came to the aid of the *Clan Chisholm* (2) in

1939 should read 20,445/1931 (page 173).

John Woodley points out that in July/August 1956 *Clan Maclean* (3) rescued the entire crew of 23 from the ketch Moyana belonging to the School of Navigation, Southampton which was beginning to break up in bad weather whilst returning home from Lisbon after winning the first Tall Ships Race.

Perhaps inevitably in a book of this size and complexity (although still a source of acute pain to its compilers), there are a number of other small typos and inconsistencies which eagle-eyed readers have pointed out to us. Whilst these are either self-evident or very minor and do not affect the work's historical accuracy, we feel that they should be corrected (we only wish other publishers would do likewise). We have therefore produced a list of them, plus some additional minor details concerning the photographs, which is available to anyone who bought 'Clan Line'. If you want a copy just write to our London address.

What is probably a tartan stem jack is being flown by *Clan Menzies* (3) berthed at Avonmouth. *[Roy Fenton collection]*

## PUTTING THE RECORD STRAIGHT

Letters, additions, amendments and photographs relating to features in any issues of 'Record' are welcomed. Communications by e-mail are acceptable, but senders are asked to include their postal address. Letters may be lightly edited.

**Manchester Prince**
In George Swaine's letter in 'Record' 38 (page 84) he is quite correct in stating that services to the Mediterranean from Manchester were not a 'joint service' of Prince Line and Manchester Liners. I feel, however, that he has omitted part of the story.

As R.B. Stoker, former Chairman and Managing Director of Manchester Liners, recounts in his book 'The Saga of Manchester Liners' (Kinglish Ltd., 1985), Prince Line, who had operated from Manchester since the opening of the Ship Canal, decided in 1968 to close the service which by then was losing money. (They were also thinking of closing the London service.)

Manchester Liners, who felt that this would be detrimental to their business, purchased the Prince Line loading brokers, Gough and Crosthwaite, gained conference rights to the Mediterranean and started their own replacement service under the name 'Manchester Prince Line'. By using small, chartered vessels and 'creaming' the trade, they were able to make this profitable.

Prior to containerisation from 1971, this service used small, conventional vessels which were renamed with Prince Line names, including the *Tartar Prince* (ex *Egret*) pictured on page 81 of 'Record' 38, the *Saxon Prince* (ex *Cairntrader*), the *Chiltern Prince* and others. Prince Line themselves adopted a similar policy in order to continue their London service.

Mr Swaine is puzzled by the presence of a 'London' ship in the Ship Canal (cover picture, 'Record' 37) and, whilst I cannot give a definite explanation, I can state (just to add to the puzzle) that Prince Line and Furness ships of the *Black Prince* size used to occasionally turn up inward bound from U.S. Gulf ports. I have further photos of the *Black Prince* taken in the Canal in 1971 and remember this being an arrival from those ports, which were a source of much traffic to the canal, carried in cargo liners of various companies.
KEN LOWE, 4 Ansells, Seaview, Isle of Wight PO34 5JL

*Lagosian* **explained**
I was interested to see mention of the *Lagosian* (ex *Melmay*) and her suggested antecedents including attributing her building at Greenock Dockyard for account of the Glasgow owner, T.L. Duff and Co. ('Record' 37, pages 56-57). Actually there is considerable earlier history involved here which will set the record straight for readers.

The first query to clear up concerns her origination as a lumber carrier. She was designed for the Dollar interests of Vancouver. Her design was influenced without doubt by the needs of the British Columbia lumber export trade from Vancouver mainly to North China and Japan. Scandinavian lumber carriers had been calling since the end of the First World War at North West Pacific ports as we call the California, Oregon, Washington and British Columbia range. Except for steam propulsion, *Melmay* was fairly typical of many Norwegian and Danish lumber carriers of the interwar years that called here to load lumber, much of it from the Canadian Robert Dollar Company's sawmill located in upper Vancouver harbour at a place then called Dollarton.

The ship was ordered by Alexander Melville Dollar, eldest son of the famous Captain Robert Dollar, for Melmay Shipping Co., a subsidiary of Canadian-American Shipping Company which had been set up by Melville around 1924. It maintained close ties with The Robert Dollar Company in San Francisco, but was independent to the extent that Melville owned it and ran his own show from Vancouver as a ship and lumber broker and shipowner having acquired three large ships from the San Francisco company between 1924 and 1928. The last of these ships was *Chief Maquilla*, ex *M.E. Dollar*, ex *War King*, which was lost in severe North Pacific conditions south of the Aleutian islands on 2nd December 1928, a matter of just a few months after acquisition.

It appears that Melville took the insurance proceeds and rolled them over into a contract for a new lumber carrier with Greenock Dockyard. The result was the *Melmay* which upset a few precedents. She was the first new building contract let by the Dollar family, all earlier ships being either second hand open market purchases or war surplus. She was also almost the only vessel not to bear the word Dollar in its name, although 'Mel' was from Melville and 'May' came from his wife's name.

A trials view of *Melmay*. [J. and M. Clarkson collection]

The depression came and Canadian-American suffered badly with a fall-off in lumber sales, deliveries by their own ships and voyage charters which were a big part of their business. In 1932 a stevedoring company petitioned Canadian-American into bankruptcy and as the owner and guarantor Melville followed. He could not get help from the San Francisco end of the family as they were by now wrestling with major problems at their own Dollar Steamship Company with its obligations involving two new President liners, *President Coolidge* and *President Harding*. Melville died by his own hand in Vancouver 1932 to be followed a month later by Captain Robert Dollar, in the latter case of natural causes. The United States press reported Melville's death as being from heart trouble, presumably in part because a suicide was likely seen as being a negative factor when the entire Dollar empire was wrestling with all sorts of difficulties of its own.

The creditors on the *Melmay* arranged to place the ship under the management of T.L. Duff and Co., shifting the domicile of the Melmay Steamship Co. Ltd. to the U.K. from Vancouver and from that point on the ship had no further connection with the Vancouver lumber trade. Duff incidentally were agents at Glasgow for Dollar Line, which suggests that there were wheels within wheels at play in the bankruptcy process. Within days of Canadian-American's failure, a new company, Anglo-Canadian Shipping, rose from the ashes headed by three senior employees of the former company. It has gone through successive ownerships, but all along it has been successful and is still in business today.
SYD HEAL, 8415 Granville Street, Box 46, Vancouver, British Columbia, Canada V6P 4Z9

**Olympian myth**
One of those lingering myths is that, when Greek Line ordered *Olympia* from Alexander Stephen in 1950, the hull had been laid down as an aircraft carrier. I suspect that this rumour is in the same category as the one that the *Queen Mary* of 1935 was to have been named *Victoria* - just a good story.

Alexander Stephen of Linthouse only ever built one aircraft carrier and that was HMS *Ocean*, one of the eleven Colossus class light fleet carriers. She had been laid down in November 1942 and was completed on 8th August 1945. The Colossus class, built to a Vickers design, were based on a relatively uncomplicated merchant ship hull so that they could be quickly built by commercial yards.

Within five months of the Second World War ending in August 1945, the Admiralty cancelled three large fleet carriers (the Malta class), two Eagle class and four Centaur class light fleet carriers: none of these had been ordered from Alexander Stephen.

Could it have been that a foreign aircraft carrier was ordered from Alexander Stephen? This seems unlikely for surplus carriers built for the United States Navy and the Royal Navy were laid up in some numbers. The emphasis in the late 1940s and into the 1950s was for British shipyards to build commercial cargo-carrying ships that owners world wide wanted and refrigerated food carriers to feed a rationed and hungry Britain. Sir Murray Alexander was busy building for the P&O Group's various subsidiaries and probably not interested in having an aircraft carrier blocking a building berth for several years. In overall length *Olympia* was 126 feet shorter than HMS *Ocean*. Not even their steam propulsion was similar: 25,000 SHP giving *Olympia* 22 knots versus 40,000 SHP producing 25 knots.

Let the myth that *Olympia* was intended as an aircraft carrier go down the Clyde on an ebb tide and be lost forever.
ANDREW BELL, Gartul, Porthleven, Cornwall TR13 9JJ

**Department of correction**
I see from my letter published in 'Record' 38, that I have managed to transpose the names of *Empire Mayring* and *Empire Maysong*. The *Empire Maysong*, of course, became MacBrayne's *Lochbroom*.
IAN RAMSAY, Garmoyle, Main Road, Langbank, Renfrewshire PA14 6XP
*Thanks to Alan Phipps who also pointed this out.*
I have a few corrections to and comments about your British and Continental fleet list in the November issue of Ships in Focus 'Record'. The list states that *Rallus* (17) was the first vessel delivered to British and Continental. In fact, that distinction falls to the next vessel in the list, *Tringa* (18). *Rallus* was first registered at London in the name of the Cork Steamship Co. Ltd., and appears as such in 'Lloyd's Register' of 1922. That explains the long gap between her launch on 1st March and her registry at Liverpool on 28th December. After the Cork Steamship Co. Ltd. was taken over by Amalgamated Industrials, its new ships were registered at London, although the company's existing ships retained their Cork registry. To be pedantic, the registry details for *Vanellus* (14), *Lestris* (15), *Ousel* (16) and *Rallus* (17) should probably show London rather than Cork after the name of the company.

A minor point of detail: the second line of the entry for *Ousel* (16) should read: O.N. 146227 1,539g 647n, rather than O.N. 1462271 539g 647n, as it actually appears.

Finally, I discovered that two ships in the fleet of F.H. Powell and Co. were registered briefly in the name of the British & Continental Steamship Co. Ltd. before being transferred to

the ownership of Alfred Henry Read. They were *Graceful* in 1909 and *Hopeful* in 1910. While there appears to be an ampersand to differentiate the two names, I wonder if any of your readers can cast any further light on that use of the name?
MALCOLM McRONALD, 4 Pear Tree Close, Heswall, Wirral, CH60 1YD.

## M for Bousses
Having been on quite a few Greek ships I think I can offer a very likely explanation for the letter M on the funnel of the ship owned by the Bousses family ('Record' 38, page 119). The Greeks do not have a letter that sounds like our B. Their B sounds like our V and indeed is pronounced Veta in the Greek alphabet. To get a sound like our B they put an M in front of a P. For instance, 'beer' would be 'mpeer', and therefore Bousses would be Mpousses. Could this be the explanation?
CRAIG CROMPTON, The Shrubs, The Street, Frampton on Severn, Gloucestershire GL2 7ED.

## *Saxon* at Millport
With reference to Ian Buxton's interesting and detailed article in 'Record' 37 about Arnott Young, I enclose a photograph of the puffer *Saxon* berthed at Millport, Isle of Cumbrae in June 1958. Readers were informed that as many as 12 puffers were broken up at Dalmuir, *Saxon* being the oldest to go, in 1967. Of 64 gross tons, her dimensions were 66.0 x 16.8 x 6.8 feet and she was built at Kirkintilloch on the Forth and Clyde Canal in 1903 by John Hay and Sons as *Dane*. For 40 years she supplied Cumbrae with coal, coming under the ownership of Walter Kerr at Millport in 1926. The 14-foot boat is tied up alongside the *Saxon* and when at sea her punt was carried on her hatch forward.
MICHAEL DICK, 6 Jacobs Drive, Gourock, Inverclyde PA19 1LH.

## Concrete evidence
Malcolm Cranfield's 'The Great Cement Armada' ('Record' 38) reminded me of the news and casualty reports which daily

*Saxon at Millport. [Michael Dick collection]*

passed before me back in 1975-76.

Elsewhere in the world, for instance the Persian Gulf, there were reports of other questionable activities. One trick was to remove the top layer of life-expired cement, replacing it with fresh before offering it for sale. A case of buyer beware. It was not easy to establish the truth of such reports.

Some of the ships were taking the opportunity of one last cargo as they headed for the scrap yard. They likely would have tired engine rooms. Who was going to spend money when they were on their last voyage? So breakdown of machinery and engine room were to be expected.

In one or two cases when anchored off Lagos or another West African port, they started to demolish the ship. In at least one case this left a hull with a dead engine room, no superstructure, masts or cargo gear on deck. How do you discharge the cargo which has set into a solid block on which bulldozers made little impression? Such ships are now local reefs.
DAVID BURRELL, 6 Glaisnock View, Cumnock, Ayrshire KA18 3GA

Malcolm Cranfield's article 'The Great Cement Armada' in 'Record' 38 has generated considerable interest and many complimentary comments. Andrew Huckett sent slides of two ships which came to grief in Nigerian waters, including one featured in Malcolm's article. *Irene's Banner* (left) was photographed on 26th September 1984. She had been beached on 22nd January 1978 after she had caught fire whilst discharging cement. *Sagittarius* (right) was photographed on 17th August 1982 at Bar Beach, Victoria Island near Lagos. She had been laid up off Lagos since 30th December 1978, and had driven aground after breaking her anchor chain on 17th February 1980. *Sagittarius* had been built in Japan during 1957 as *Okishima Maru*, and had also carried the names *Tolofon* and *Paraskevi H*. Her last owner was Stelios N. Characoglou who since 1969 had traded out of Piraeus as Jacaranda Lines S.A. Perhaps not surprisingly, *Sagittarius* was his last ship.

**An Irish armada**
Malcolm Cranfield's fascinating article ('Record' 38) reminded me of the strange events around many small ports in Ireland in the spring and early summer of 1970. Irish Cement, monopoly suppliers of the material in the Republic of Ireland, was shut down by a four-month strike which threatened the livelihoods of up to 15,000 building trade workers. Imported cement began to come in at small, quiet ports across the border in Northern Ireland, hopefully away from dockers' unions and Irish Cement pickets. The first cargo I believe came to Bangor from Runcorn on Coppack's *Vauban*, but soon Kilkeel, closer to the border, was visited by the Irish *Arklow* and *Murell*, and the Dutch *Grada Westers* and *Nomadisch*, all from Ardrossan. By early May as the strike's effects spread, much greater amounts were coming in, and the first cargoes started arriving at harbours in the far south west of Ireland, when the Dutch *Canada* brought several consignments to Baltimore and Kinsale, from Briton Ferry and Garston. County Down harbours were still busiest and the real hub was the fishing village of Ardglass, which normally only saw the occasional coaster to load barrels of fish for Holland. There was hectic activity not seen before or since. On one occasion there were six coasters in the harbour together: the British *Isle of Harris*, the Dutch *Spray*, *Bierum*, *Procyon* and *Pial*, and the German *Gesine P*. The cement was obtained wherever possible – these coasters had come from Glasgow, Fleetwood, Mostyn and even Rye in Sussex. Also trading regularly to Ardglass from Portpatrick in Scotland was the 'puffer' *Eldesa*, which many years later as the *Eilean Eisdeal* became the last of her type in service. Kilkeel (Dutch *Fiducia II*, *Trio* and locally-owned *Lady Hyacinth* ex *Ballyedward*) and also Killyleagh in Strangford Lough (*Bierum*, Dutch *Lien*) were receiving cement, quite a few cargoes all the way from Boulogne, but the brokers were busier than ever fixing cement cargoes for West Cork. The tiny Kilmacsimon Quay, up the River Bandon from Kinsale, saw the *Canada* from Briton Ferry and the British *Tower Venture* from Mistley, but it was Baltimore, not normally a commercial harbour at all, at which coasters were constantly berthing by June 1970; mainly Dutch, including the *Aurora*, *Trio*, *Ferocia* and *Netty*, while nearby Courtmacsherry saw the Dutch *Schokland* and *Rapid* among others. At the end of June it all stopped with the British *Rye Trader* and the Danish *N.O. Petersen* seemingly the last of the armada when they unloaded at Ardglass.

No doubt persons unknown made lots of money out of this 'blackleg' cement phenomenon – but it did no harm to the diminishing numbers of small coasters and small harbours!

IAN WILSON, 8 Warren Road, Donaghadee BT21 0DS

Diesel-engined Clyde 'puffer' *Eldesa*, previously *VIC 72*, discharging cement at Ardglass, County Down in June 1970. *[Ian Wilson collection]*

# RECORD REVIEWS

**ARMED MERCHANT CRUISERS 1878-1945**
**By Richard Osborne, Harry Spong and Tom Grover**
**328-page A4 hardback published by the World Ship Society Ltd. at £45.00**

Armed merchant cruisers were mostly substantial passenger liners which were commissioned into the Royal Navy to stand in for major warships, often seeing arduous service. So, spanning as they do both mercantile and naval history, why have these ships not received the coverage they deserve? Examining this book shows why: to do the subject justice this book required a huge amount of research, and an appreciation of both naval procedures and merchant ship operation.

The text is divided into four parts. The first tells of the Admiralty's experience with the *Hecla*, bought in 1878 whilst fitting out at Belfast and completed as a cruiser-torpedo depot ship to gain experience with merchant ship conversions. The next part deals with development of policy concerning armed merchant cruisers between 1878 and 1914, and gives details of the 16 vessels taken up for conversion during a scare about a war with Russia in 1885. Data in these entries in this and subsequent chapters include most of that expected in a fleet list entry, but with a concentration on naval service. Part three covers the First World War. This covers naval operations carried out by armed merchant cruisers, notably their arduous work on the Northern patrol lines which imposed the blockade on Germany with important consequences for the eventual outcome of the conflict. The fourth and longest section concerns the Second World War, recording that most of the ships taken up as armed merchant cruisers were eventually used, probably more usefully, as troop carriers. As well as operational details, this section contains much on aspects such as manning, armament, electronic equipment, aircraft carried and fuel. For both wars, details and careers of all British armed merchant cruisers are included.

With the help of extensive quotes from Admiralty documents a good impression is given of the official view of the usefulness of armed merchant cruisers. Particularly telling is the authors' comparison of the British ships with the smaller but generally fast and better armed merchant vessels which the Germans used as commerce raiders.

The aim of writing the definitive work on the British armed merchant cruisers has been fully achieved in 'Armed Merchant Cruisers', and this book is likely to remain the last word on the policy of using such ships, their equipment and service. Indeed, there is little one could wish to know on the subject that is not included.

The question of whether the book offers value for money depends on whether the reader is a World Ship Society member or not. The Society has a policy of pricing books 50% higher to non-members, and this makes 'Armed Merchant Cruisers' expensive to them, although good value to members. The WSS needs to consider whether the high price of books to non-members is actually damaging its overall sales.

The recent merchant ship publications of the World Ship Society have been criticised for poor production values, perhaps the low point being one in which many images had been downloaded from the Web. The Society's warship publications have generally been better. However, it must be said that the material, the authors' work and the photographs in 'Armed Merchant Cruisers' does deserve something a little better. Paper quality and reproduction are generally excellent, but the cover design is dull and the photographs are reproduced to several different sizes, some surrounded by white space and some not. This does not detract from the value of the material therein, but with more effort – and the services of someone with design flair – the book's appearance could have matched its first class content.

Roy Fenton

**OCEAN LINER TWILIGHT Steaming to adventure 1968-1979**
**By Theodore W. Scull**
**128 page softback   217 x 280mm   published by Overview Press Limited at £16.00**

Ted Scull, a pre-eminent shipping and travel writer based in New York, has dipped into his diaries and written 'Ocean Liner Twilight'. Hugely well-travelled, Ted Scull voyages on ships ranging from trans-Atlantic liners that are known to all to the last ship in British India's once large fleet. Interweaved into some adventurous voyaging are trips bravely made on passenger trains which even the most enterprising of travel agent would not have known about.

The book is lavishly illustrated with well-produced colour photos mainly taken by the author. So numerous are they that some of the ships in them get no mention in the text, but they look nice anyway. Some pictures are questionably duplicated such as *Canberra* diverted via a wintery Cape Town and partly obscured by a smokey tug. *S.A. Vaal* is twice shown alongside in Las Palmas. This book is a passenger's experience of ships and, perhaps disappointingly, it is not a shipping book. The author could be said to be the star rather than the ships themselves. Few technical details get a mention: why ships were shaped by their trade routes or what cargoes they carried: perhaps all this was not recorded in the Scull diaries. The book is not a must in a shipping collection but nevertheless it is a pleasurable romp across the seven seas that we could not do now and as such is an enjoyable chronicle. It is well produced by Bill Mayes as publisher.

Andrew Bell

**MERSEYSIDE MARITIME RESEARCH**
**Another collection of research papers from the Liverpool Nautical Research Society to celebrate the Society's seventieth anniversary 1938-2008**
**74-page softback published by the Liverpool Nautical Research Society at £5.00**

The Liverpool Nautical Research Society are to be congratulated, both on reaching 70 years and on publishing a collection of research papers which exhibit such a diversity of interests and abilities amongst its membership. 'Merseyside Maritime Research' can hold its head up amongst academically-inclined journals in covering a wide field of research. To start with there is a sympathetic but revealing portrait of a significant member of the ship owning Harrison family, a welcome history of Stuart and Douglas who were significant Liverpool ship owners from the days of sail, an account of the once-important north west port of Ulverstone, and brief histories of some the marine insurance companies established in Liverpool. James Pottinger contributes amusing but thoughtful recollections of some of the engineers he served with in Brocklebank ships, there is a history of the Liverpool institutions which trained wireless operators, a detailed account of how the patent log was developed, and survivors' stories of the loss of the *Western Prince* of 1929. Although relatively short, the review of the introduction of steam at sea is a remarkably comprehensive list of early attempts to harness steam for propulsion. The only contribution which covers familiar ground is a description of the merger of Cunard and White Star, which does not originate within the Society but won its 2004 prize for a student essay.

This reviewer has but two niggles. Firstly, sources are listed for most articles, the most notable omission being the review of steam at sea which – given the extent of the author's researches – is crying out for such a list. Secondly, certain contributors have been allowed to get away with not explaining the abstruse technical terms they use. For instance, who beyond the world of radio operators knows what is a 'coherer-receiver' (page 40)?

The book is printed on good quality paper which reproduces well the illustrations, which have obviously been chosen or drawn with care, and it is very reasonably priced. It is a collection of which the Liverpool Nautical Research Society can be proud.

Roy Fenton

**COASTER PHOTOGRAPHS AT THE PORT OF WELLS-NEXT-THE-SEA 1970s - 1980s**
**No author given.**
**A4 softback, 80 pages, published by Dawrich Publishers, King's Lynn at £12.50**

I am not a writer, have never done a review and was brought up to believe that if you can't say something good it is better to say nothing.

Well, the cover looks attractive, the printer has used a decent paper and there is an excellent statement on the inside of the front cover 'wish we had more like this photograph' with which I completely agree.

What happened to pages 1 and 2 I don't know as we begin on page 3. Problems continue with the layout of the introduction - sometimes there is a line between paragraphs, sometimes not. An editor with a knowledge of the English language would have been a help. Several of the ships' names are spelt wrong, page 47 *'Vaughbon'* is actually *Vauban*, and *'Petite Fulmar'* should be *Petit Folmer* on page 31. Many of the photographs are grainey, see the *Pavo* on page 65, and some are way off sharp - top of pages 80 and 81. A lot of the ships are cropped, not only masts but some have lost their bows or sterns. In this reviewer's opinion the overlaying of one picture on top of another is not a good idea but to plaster the ship's name, in a green box, across a picture leaves me cold. Why use a back-lit photograph of the *Ni-Tricia* (page 60) when there are much better views of her assisting ships in other photos and as for the small photo of *Niagara* on page 51 well... As for captions, whilst I prefer a well written descriptive caption I don't have problem with a box giving basic details of the subject of the photo but all should be treated the same way - captions or data and all must have a description of some sort.

Having said all that the book will not appear in Book List 39 but if anyone would like a copy we do have a few available.

John Clarkson.

# DR WILLIAM LIND
## Archivist extraordinaire 1931-2007

After a short illness, William Lind, as the progenitor and driving force behind the archive work of The Ballast Trust, died peacefully on 22nd October 2007.

In practical terms the full extent of the business records that he saved for the nation would be difficult to quantify, but certainly includes a wealth of Clydeside shipbuilding, engineering, railway and other industrial company archives including irreplaceable drawings, photographs and models, some dating back to the nineteenth century which otherwise would have been lost for ever.

Bill Lind was born in Johnstone, Renfrewshire, in 1931 as the eldest of three sons and the only one to follow his father in the contracting and quarrying family firm of that same name which was established in 1910. He was educated at Merchiston Castle boys' school in Edinburgh, and in 1947 set out to gain practical training as a shipwright with James Lamont and Co. Ltd. in Port Glasgow.

At that time Lamonts had a three-berth shipbuilding yard and two repair slipways at Port Glasgow in addition to a dry dock and extensive repair facilities at East India Harbour in Greenock. They were building five river craft for the Irrawaddy Flotilla Company and three motor coasters for Norwegian owners. On the repair side they handled all manner of vessels including those of MacBraynes, the Caledonian Steam Packet Company, coasters, tugs, Scottish fishery protection vessels and conversions of LCTs and LSTs into commercial vessels. His training would have been very extensive.

In 1949, however, Bill was called up under the National Service scheme and was able to apply his inherited family interest in commercial vehicles with the Royal Army Service Corps, being commissioned with the post of adjutant before demobilisation but then continued to serve with the Territorials until retiring in 1972, and thereafter served as a member of the Regular Services Resettlement Committee for Scotland.

*The formal Dr William Lind (left) from twenty years ago and Bill, the friendly, helpful gentleman (right) many of us came to know and respect.*

From 1951 to 1987 he was heavily involved, first with his father in the by then seven-quarry business of Wm. Lind and Co. Ltd., whose prominent slate-grey trucks with red lettering were a familiar sight in central Scotland, and later with associated companies including W.H.Malcolm until he sold out his remaining interests in the business to that same company.

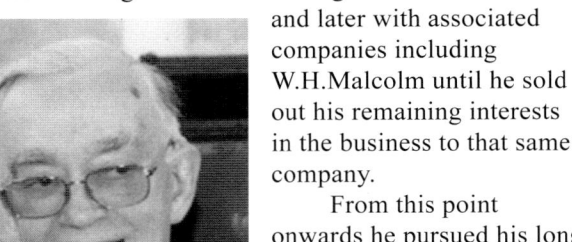

From this point onwards he pursued his long-term interest in industrial history by establishing the Aggregate Foundation to help Glasgow University provide a Centre for Business History in Scotland, which was in fact the first of its kind in Britain. In recognition of this valuable work the honorary degree of Doctor of Laws was conferred upon him by Glasgow University in 1988.

Two years after giving up the quarry and contracting business he endowed The Ballast Trust as the very fine technical archive service in Johnstone that we know today, linked as it is to the Centre for Business History at the University. In the 18 years of its existence under Bill Lind, the Trust has made appraisals, listings and given temporary storage to vast quantities of industrial records which must have begun with the closure of the Scott Lithgow complex at that time, and has continued with many other companies, including even the Port Glasgow and Newark Sailcloth Company with records dating back to the nineteenth century.

Bill was happily married for 45 years, but through growing infirmity his wife predeceased him in 2001. He was a most efficient and quietly independent gentleman with a great sense of humour and strongly held views. He will forever be long remembered not only for creating The Ballast Trust and its premises, but ensuring the necessary in-house skills were in place for processing the precious irreplaceable records which are thereby saved for the benefit of present and future generations to come.

Archie D. Munro

Not only did The Ballast Trust rescue technical information and company archives but also ensured the safety of collections of photographs and negatives, from both corporate sources and private photographers. Included in the latter was the collection of Dan MacDonald from which a few examples have been chosen.

Appropriate to this issue of 'Record' is this view of Dalmuir Basin taken on 7th June 1953. The incomplete cruiser *Tiger,* finally commissioned in 1959, is on the left, with the liners *Mahana* (8,740/1917), newly arrived, and the *Chitral* (15,346/1925) next to the quay on which demolition has started. *[Negative 967]*

Photographed on 10th July 1952 (top left) is the Steel and Bennie tug *Strongbow* (197/1927) still fitted with the wireless equipment which had been widely used when towing sailing ships such as the *L'Avenir* in pre-war days. *[Negative 0-124]*

The bow of Finnish barque *L'Avenir* (top right) (2,754/1908) in Princes Dock, Glasgow on 10th July 1934. Note the embellishments and the crew painting overside from stages. *[Negative 1908-13]*

Donaldson's *Dorelian* (6,431/1923) (middle) being canted in Princes Dock by the Clyde Shipping tugs *Flying Falcon* (283/1934) and *Flying Eagle* (260/1928) on 25th October 1947. *[Negative 934]*

The puffer *Pibroch* (bottom) was completed in 1923 as the *Texa* and is shown at Dunardry, eastbound in the Crinan Canal on 4th June 1950. *Pibroch* was renamed *Cumbrae Lass* in 1957 and ended her days at Dalmuir, arrriving there in August 1967. *[Negative 329]*

# A FORT AGAINST THE RISING SUN
## Malcolm Cooper

It was very rare for a Second World War Allied merchant ship to survive torpedo damage on two separate occasions. The Canadian-built war standard *Fort Camosun* was unique in that her assailant on both occasions was a Japanese submarine, the first of which attacked her quite literally a few hours into her maiden voyage. While the Imperial Navy had a large and modern submarine fleet, it was largely deployed in support of fleet operations, and only a fraction of its vessels spent any significant time waging war on commerce.

The *Fort Camosun* was one of the earliest of the North Sands-type standard ships to leave the building yard. Named fittingly after an early trading post in Victoria, British Columbia, she was completed by the Victoria Machinery Depot Co. Ltd. (Yard No. 20) on 2nd June 1942. She sailed independently from Victoria on her maiden voyage at 08.20 on 19th June, bound initially for Panama with a cargo of 9,000 tons of lumber, wheat, lead and zinc, and a crew of 51 (including four Canadian gunners) under the command of Captain T.F. Eggleston.

At 22.45 on the same day she was steaming south at 10 knots in position 47.22 north by 125.30 west off the north Washington state coast when she was hit by a torpedo on the port side under the bridge, the torpedo itself only being seen from the bridge by the third officer a few seconds before the explosion blew off the hatches on number 2 hold and broke the chains securing the fore deck cargo. Due to the strike taking place abreast the bulkhead between numbers 2 and 3 holds, the damage was widespread and potentially fatal. The holds in question flooded immediately through the 40 by 30 foot hole, quickly followed by number 1 hold whose aft bulkhead had been torn by the force of the blast and by the stokehold. The engines were stopped immediately and the vessel settled by the head with a heavy list to port.

There was every reason to believe that the *Fort Camosun* was doomed, and at 23.00 the master ordered the vessel to be abandoned using the two starboard boats (the port pair having been destroyed by the explosion). Two naval ratings were thought to be missing, but were found sound asleep in their bunks when the vessel, which showed no signs of sinking, was briefly re-boarded at 23.45. Clearly the large lumber component in the cargo was helping keep the vessel afloat, but an inspection by the chief engineer showed that water had reached the furnace doors in the stokehold, extinguishing the fires, and the crew were quickly ordered back into the boats. No sooner had the boats pulled away than the submarine started shelling the ship from the starboard beam. Due to the dark, the lifeboat occupants saw only the flashes of two shells but not the submarine itself. One of these shells hit on the starboard waterline at the cross bunkers, causing the ship to settle further but to right herself. After this brief assault, there was no further sign of the enemy, who probably thought that the ship was bound to sink.

The boats lay off the wallowing *Fort Camosun* throughout the night. At five in the morning a US patrol plane appeared, followed by two others, which circled the ship. At 09.00 the Canadian corvettes HMCS *Quesnel* and HMCS *Edmundson* appeared, dropping depth charges which almost blew the men out of the boats. The former picked up all survivors at 09.45, transferring the deck crew to her sister 15 minutes later. At 11.50 the deck crew and chief engineer re-boarded their ship, which the master no longer believed to be sinking, and at 12.30 the *Edmundson* took her under tow. However, the *Fort Camosun* was well down by the head, drawing about 40 feet forward, and the tow was abandoned just before two in the afternoon when she became unmanageable in a heavy swell. Salvage operations were resumed at 17.40 when the *Edmundson* secured alongside to rig emergency pumps and jettison foredeck cargo.

Eventually a combination of three US tugs, the *Dauntless*, *Henry Foss* and *Tantunk*, and the salvage vessel *Salvage Queen* got the ship around Cape Flattery into Neah Bay where she moored at 18.00 on the 21st. Here temporary patches were secured over the holes in the hull and the ship pumped dry, before she was towed to Esquimalt for permanent repairs.

The *Fort Camosun* had been unlucky enough to encounter Commander Meiji Tagami's *I-25*, one of a pair of Japanese submarines making a rare foray off America's northern Pacific coast. *I-25*'s sister *I-26* had sunk the United States freighter *Coast Trader* south west of Cape Flattery on 7th June. Apart from this, and the damage to the Fort, the two vessels' only other contribution to the war came when *I-25*, having attacked but missed two other vessels on the 21st, ineffectually shelled Fort Stevens, Oregon, and when *I-26* attacked the Estevan Point lighthouse and radio station on Vancouver Island on 20th June with similar lack of success.

After repairs and the long passage to the east coast via the Panama Canal, the *Fort Camosun* finally sailed for the UK with convoy HX.215, departing New York on 11th November 1942 and arriving in the Mersey on 25th November after an uneventful crossing. One of the peculiarities of the Ocean and Fort-type standard ships built in North America was that they sailed from their builders under provisional registry only, and did not formally enter the British register

The tug *Henry Foss* closes in on the *Fort Camosun*. [Vancouver Maritime Museum 12109]

The salvage vessel *Salvage Queen* trying to get a line aboard. [V.M.M. 12119]

Bow on with salvage vessels on her port side. [V.M.M.12110]

Fort Camosun with the Salvage Queen alongside. [V.M.M.12120]

Resting on the bottom in Neah Bay. [V.M.M.12118]

Under tow again in Neah Bay. [V.M.M.12152]

with an Official Number until after they had arrived in the UK (by contrast, most of the Park standard ships were registered in Canada before departure). Thus the *Fort Camosun* only entered the register at London on 3rd December 1942 in the name of the Ministry of War Transport, with management entrusted to T. and J. Brocklebank. In common with 89 other Forts, she was actually only on bare boat charter to the Ministry of War Transport. Her real owner was the United States War Shipping Administration, to which she had been sold in a purely financial transaction under the Hyde Park Agreement,

The *Fort Camosun* sailed again from Liverpool on 27th December with ON.157 – although initially bound for New York, her final destination was actually South Africa. In December 1943 the ship was operating in the Indian Ocean when she had her second damaging encounter with the Imperial Japanese submarine force, this time in the guise of Commander Toshiaki Fukumura's *I-27*. This submarine had already sunk another Fort standard, the *Fort Mumford*, 500 miles north west of Ceylon on 20th March 1943. On that occasion, Fukumura had complied with official policy concerning the fate of survivors and had machine-gunned the crew, leaving only one survivor, a gunner, to be rescued by Arab dhow. The *Fort Camosun* was to be far luckier.

Before she encountered the *Fort Camosun* the *I-27* had sunk four vessels in the Gulf of Aden and the Arabian Sea, the Liberties *Sambo* and *Sambridge* on 10th and 18th November, and the Greek freighters *Athina Livanos* and *Nitsa* on 29th November and 2nd December. The *Fort Camosun*, now under the command of Captain R. Humble, had sailed independently from Vizagapatam for Aden on 22nd November with a cargo of 7,900 tons of Indian produce and a crew of 89, of whom 59 were lascars and 30 (including four army and five navy gunners) were British. She had proceeded without incident until 23.15 on 3rd December when, zig-zagging at 11 knots in position 11.23 north by 46.03 east, she was struck by a torpedo on the port side aft just forward of the bulkhead between numbers 4 and 5 holds. Although the weather was fine and visibility good, it was very dark and nothing was seen either of her assailant or the torpedo track.

Number 4 lower hold, loaded with jute, gunny, peanuts and sandbags, flooded immediately after the violent explosion, which blew off the hatch covers and destroyed number 6 boat. Apart from a fire in the 'tween deck and a local failure of the chartroom and compass lights, however, there was little other material damage. The ship heeled to starboard with the explosion, shuddered violently for a few seconds and then slowly righted herself. Captain Humble quickly came to the view that the *Fort Camosun* was in no danger and swung the vessel four points to starboard (away from the presumed position of the enemy submarine on the port quarter), ordering the crew to action stations as he did so.

The vessel's engines stopped for 10 minutes due to a temporary breakdown in communication between bridge and engine room, but within another 10 minutes the vessel was proceeding at good speed without ever having lost way. During this time, the remaining port lifeboats left the ship without permission, number 4 with its correct complement of 19 and number 2 with only four lascar seamen. The master did not consider it safe to stop, and so left the lifeboats to their fate. It subsequently emerged that when the quartermaster in charge of numbers 4 and 6 boats got on deck, he saw that number 6 had gone, assumed that it had left as per orders and acted accordingly. No blame was subsequently attached to any of those involved – the quartermaster himself had already been torpedoed four times during the war, while a number of the other departees had come from ships with standing orders to abandon ship if torpedoed.

Beyond the lifeboat incident, there were few serious problems. The fire was extinguished by 02.00 and, although it subsequently re-started twice, it never posed a real threat to the vessel's survival. An escort vessel, detached from an outward-bound convoy, came to the *Fort Camosun's* assistance just as the fire was being extinguished, but Captain Humble reported that he could proceed unaided at 8½ knots and directed the would be rescuers to search for the lifeboats astern. Number 5 bulkhead was inspected at 10.30 and water was found to be seeping through several rivets and seams. Although concerned that the bulkhead might give way if the jute in the hold began to swell, the master did not think the water was entering the hold very quickly and held his course for Aden, arriving there at 15.00 on 4th December, drawing 30 feet aft with 17 feet of water in number 5 hold. By this time the men left behind in the boats had already been picked up by HMS *Bann*. Subsequently transferred to HMS *Carnatic*, they were landed at Aden on the 6th.

While the *Fort Camosun* had been in real danger of sinking after her first brush with the enemy, this was never the case with the second attack. Although there was no material for repairs at Aden, the crew managed to patch the hole in the hull using hatch and tank top ceiling boards. Although there was some slight leakage in heavy weather in the Atlantic on the way home to the UK for permanent repairs, the ship reached Loch Ewe safely early in 1944.

Japan's submarine fleet was almost completely destroyed during the last two years of the war, and neither of the *Fort Camosun's* attackers was among the handful of vessels to survive. *I-25* had already gone by the time her sister made her attack. Nothing was heard of her after a reconnaissance report sent from off Espiritu Santo Island on 24th August 1943, and she was almost certainly the victim of a depth charge attack by destroyer, either USS *Patterson* on 25th August or USS *Ellet* on 3rd September. *I-27*, easily the most successful of Japan's submarine fleet in terms of Allied merchant ships sunk, did not long survive her December 1943 encounter the *Fort Camosun*. Perhaps fittingly, she went down in a blaze of glory at the hands of Royal Navy destroyers in her very next attack. Having sunk the troopship *Khedive Ismail* with the loss of over 1,000 soldiers and crew in an attack on a convoy off the Maldives on 12th February 1944, she was blown to the surface by the escorting destroyers HMS *Paladin* and HMS *Petard*. The submarine was then smothered in gunfire, but 4-inch high explosive shells did little real damage to her pressure hull, and an attempt to ram by the *Paladin* did more damage to the British vessel than to the Japanese. *I-27* was only finally sent to the bottom when *Petard* achieved a rare reversal of roles and sank her at the 7th torpedo attempt. She went down with 99 hands, leaving only the 100th to be picked up by the British.

In contrast, the *Fort Camosun's* history after her second Japanese submarine encounter was completely devoid of drama. She operated without further incident under the British flag until late 1947. She was then returned to US ownership, now in the guise of the United States Maritime Commission. A total of 68 Forts were thus treated, and although 18 were sold on to the Italian government and returned to commercial service, the remainder went straight into mothballs and did not sail again. The *Fort Camosun* was in the latter group and remained at her moorings until the early part of 1960, when she was sold to the Commercial Metals Company of Dallas and broken up.

*Fort Camosun* on 9th November 1942 just before her long-delayed maiden passage to the United Kingdom. *[Ian J. Farquhar]*